*One of the Greatest
Love Stories
of the Century*

It began with a telephone call to an apartment shared by four bachelor girls near Buckingham Palace.

The call was from the Palace itself — an invitation from Queen Elizabeth II of England asking nineteen-year-old Lady Diana Spencer to be a weekend guest at the British Royal Family's Scottish home, Balmoral Castle.

Three days later, as they walked beside a woodland stream, Prince Charles and Lady Diana paused, looked into each others' eyes, and knew that something very special had begun.

Six months would pass before they officially announced their love to the world. This is their story...the story of two extraordinary people and a very special romance...for all the world to share in every beautiful detail.

Charles and Diana

A ROYAL ROMANCE

by Janice Dunlop

5578

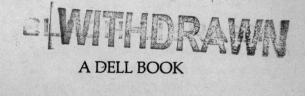

A DELL BOOK

Published by
Dell Publishing Co., Inc.
1 Dag Hammarskjold Plaza
New York, New York 10017

Dell® TM 681510, Dell Publishing Co., Inc.

ISBN 0-440-11205-2

Printed in the United States of America

First printing—May 1981

Contents

Sir Winston Churchill
1620-1688

KING CHARLES II
1630-1685
& Lucy Walters

John
1st Duke of
Marlborough
1650-1722

Mrs. Mary Sarsfield

Anne
Countess of
Sunderland
(d. 1716)

Mrs. Charlotte Vesey

Hon. John Spencer
of Althorp
1708-1746

Anne
Lady Bingham
(d. 1761)

John
1st Earl Spencer
1734-1783

Charles
1st Earl of Lucan
1735-1799

George John
2nd Earl Spencer
1758-1834

Lady Lavinia Bingham
1762-1831

Frederick
4th Earl Spencer
1798-1857

LINEAGE
Lady Diana Frances Spencer

Elizabeth Sarah Lavinia
1955-

KING CHARLES II
1630-1685
& Barbara Villiers
|
Henry
1st Duke of
Grafton
1563-1690
|
Charles
2nd Duke of
Grafton
1683-1757
|
Isabella
Marchioness of
Hertford
1726-1782
|
Admiral Hugh Seymour ▬▬▬▬▬▬
1759-1801

JAMES II
1633-1701
& Arabella, daughter of
Sir Winston Churchill
|
Henrietta
Baroness Waldegrave
1699-1730
|
James
1st Earl of
Waldegrave
(d. 1741)
|
James
2nd Earl of
Waldegrave
1715-1763
|
Anna Horatia
(d. 1801)

Sir Horace Beauchamp
Seymour
1791-1856
|
▬▬▬ Adelaide Horatia Seymour
1825-1877

Charles Robert
6th Earl Spencer
1857-1922
|
Albert Edward John ▬▬▬▬▬▬▬   Cynthia Eleanor Hamilton
7th Earl Spencer   (b. 1897)
(b. 1892)

Edward John ▬▬▬▬▬▬▬   Hon. Frances Roche
8th Earl Spencer   1936-
1924-   (div)

Cynthia Jane   Diana Frances   Charles Edward Maurice
1957-   1961-   Viscount Althorp
                                       1964-

Charles
and
Diana

A ROYAL ROMANCE

I

A Telephone Rings

The shrill sound of the telephone bell cut across the girlish clamor in the apartment block first-floor flat overlooking Old Brompton Road, a pleasant enough but undistinguished shopping street nicely placed less than two miles from the tourist sights of Buckingham Palace and a convenient ten-minute brisk walk from Knightsbridge and the world-famous top people's store, Harrods.

Phone calls always caused excitement at number 60 Coleherne Court. When girls leave home for the first time to share a flat together in a big city, the telephone becomes their link to the outside world full of single men.

Through that cream instrument on the small table in the lofty but rather gloomy hallway would come, they hoped, the invitations to dinner, to

11

weekends in the country, the prospect of love, romance, even marriage.

In this crowded three-bedroom flat shared by four girls, all in their late teens or early twenties, the phone was constantly in use, particularly in the evenings. It had been installed in the hall so that each of the girls, who had been living together for just over a year, would have some degree of privacy for their giggly chats and whispered confidences.

Not that there were any secrets between these four who had left home to find excitement in London. They shared each other's happiness and interest over new boyfriends and the tears and brief despair over shattered romances. But most of all their small world rang with the sound of the laughter they shared. The noise from number 60 was always at a high decibel level.

Dark-haired Virginia Pitman aged twenty-one, the noisiest and most extroverted of the "famous four"—a name from the Enid Blyton stories they had all read as children—was the first to reach the phone. "373-7462," said Virginia. After listening, there was an uncharacteristic frown across her forehead as she put the receiver down on the recently polished surface of the telephone table and went into the cluttered but—considering the close proximity of four young women—reasonably tidy living room.

In this flat there was a rotating system and all the girls had their housekeeping jobs to do. "Diana, it's for you," Virginia told the organizer of the rotation, a blonde in jeans and sweater who owned the £1000,000 flat. "It's some man who says he is from Buckingham Palace: it must be his idea of a joke."

The blonde strode across to the phone. "Yes, this is Diana Spencer." She listened for about a minute with only the occasional "yes" and "I understand," but when she put the phone back on the hook, she was flushed with pleasure. The news she had to tell Virginia and her two other flatmates, Ann Bolton and Carolyn Pride, made all the girls shriek with excitement. The girl the others jokingly called the "landlady" had been invited to spend the weekend at Balmoral, the British Royal Family's Scottish Castle.

Anne, Virginia, and Carolyn, all very well-brought-up young ladies from the top drawer of English aristocracy with cut-glass crystal accents, did not need to be told who or what Balmoral was. But they all realized what such an invitation meant in the complex pecking order of the English upper classes.

Two days later Diana was standing in a line at Heathrow, the huge international airport twenty miles down the traffic-choked M4 motorway from her flat in the London postal district of SW5. The name on her ticket just read Miss D. Spencer and the passenger list for the British Airways flight gave no clues to the small knot of keen-eyed, rather scruffily dressed men waiting at the entrance to the departure gate in the ultramodern number one terminal building.

The date was September 5, 1980, and nineteen-year-old Diana, a kindergarten teacher, fresh out of school herself, was off on a rendez-vous that would change the life of this girl who was born a lady but was destined to become a princess and one day a queen.

The keen-eyed men at the gate were journalists based at the busiest international airport in the world, and they were on the lookout for a blonde. Their eyes flickered across the thick, well-brushed tresses of the girl who clutched her ticket and a small brown leather overnight bag.

''No, that's not her,'' said burly Ray Watts, an experienced old hand at spotting the one face among the thousands who flood through Heath-row every day. This group of five men—one other reporter besides Ray and three photographers, Nikons and flash guns always at the ready—were looking for one blonde in particular.

Ray clutched a newspaper clipping with a creased picture of a stunningly beautiful woman, so obviously more sophisticated and glamorous than the Miss D. Spencer in the line he had ignored. The newspapermen were eager for a piece for the morning-paper gossip columns, a lucrative bit of scandal about the latest episode in the continuingly ever more complex love life of the thirty-one-year-old bachelor heir to the En-glish throne.

The same passenger list that bore the name D. Spencer also carried a D. Sheffield, a significant name and destination on that cool September afternoon toward the end of a wet and miserable summer. It was common knowledge that the ups and downs of the dashing Prince Charming's much-reported love life had reached a low ebb.

He was in Balmoral, just fifty miles from the destination of this flight . . . the bustling oil-rich city of Aberdeen in northern Scotland, on holiday in the royal country estate, and the bunch of journalists knew that he was a creature of habit, quite likely to invite a beautiful young woman to share a holiday weekend.

The name Sheffield looked like a winner. Davina Sheffield had easily been the prettiest of the Prince's long collection of lovely women companions. It was well known that although their twelve-month romance had ended some eighteen months previously, the two had kept in touch.

The Fleet Street mass-selling newspapers, the *Daily Express*, *Daily Star*, and *The Sun*, had told how the Prince had fallen out with the latest of his conquests and had gone to Balmoral; and what better than an old flame to fill the void and brighten up a long, lonely weekend.

So the Heathrow press crew ignored the unknown Miss D. Spencer as she boarded the British Airways Trident jet for the two-hour flight to Aberdeen. The events of the forthcoming weekend would make them curse with frustration when they realized what they had missed. But Diana herself would have been surprised if they had taken her photograph because, as far as she was concerned, she had been invited to Balmoral by Queen Elizabeth II for a friendly, informal family weekend. She didn't know who had prompted the invitation because he wanted to meet again the lovely schoolgirl whom he was later to tell the world he only remembered as "a splendid girl, so full of fun."

But neither Prince Charles or Diana could have dreamt that less than twenty-four hours later they would both suddenly realize they were in love . . . a love that sparked off a whirlwind courtship and ended with a Buckingham Palace candlelight-supper marriage proposal just six months later.

The most eligible bachelor in the world would fall helplessly in love with an attractive, blue-eyed teen-ager, hardly out of school and twelve years his junior.

Diana was born with a title, a real-life Lady with a position of privilege, but nevertheless a child of our times, a product of a broken home, her family separated by divorce.

Overnight, with the stroke of a pen, she would become a member of the Royal Family and be called Princess of Wales, Countess of Chester, Duchess of Cornwall, Duchess of Rothesay, Countess of Carrick, and Baroness Renfrew.

She would inherit enormous wealth and power and one day be crowned Queen of England.

Diana and Charles's love story would become the romance of the century.

It was dark when the Trident touched down at Dyce, Aberdeen's airport, once a sleepy terminal with just a couple of flights a day but now grown to handle the traffic generated by the North Sea oil finds. Lady Diana joined the hundred or so other passengers, mostly workers heading back for another hard two-month spell on the rigs battered by endless northern gales or dark-suited businessmen with fat briefcases off to clinch another deal involving Britain's substantial "black gold" undersea discoveries.

Just as at Heathrow, 514 miles away, Dyce Airport had its passenger watchers too. Two Scottish photographers from the *Daily Express* and the *Daily Mail*. They also missed the blond Lady Diana. In her below knee-length fashionable dark gray skirt and light blue windbreaker she looked just like any of the local girls, dressed against what passed for summer this far north. That afternoon it had rained in Aberdeen, nothing unusual for Scotland; mist and cloud were part of the country's attractions.

The bracing climate had been the delight of generations of hardy Royals who had made Royal Deeside into their traditional summer retreat since the days of Queen Victoria, whose beloved Prince Albert had designed the castle to resemble a schloss on the Rhine. The present Royal Family has carried on in the tradition of enjoying the exhilaration of early-morning horseback gallops across heather-covered moorland, grouse shoots, and icy fishing expeditions for the silver salmon leaping from the fast flowing waters of the Dee.

One airport watcher, blending in among the locals in green waterproof anorak, tweed suit, and sensible walking shoes, spotted Diana, however.

This man was in his late twenties, well spoken, quiet, and unassuming. Under his jacket he wore a fully loaded .38 caliber revolver in a soft leather holster. He was one of the thirty or so Royal Detectives, handpicked by Scotland Yard to protect the top ten members of the British Royal Family.

The gun guard round the Royals, particularly Prince Charles, had in the past always been very low key. But the assassination by the Irish Republican Army of the Prince's uncle, Lord Louis Mountbatten, the previous year had changed all that.

Now all the Royals and even their guests were protected by these young Scotland Yard men rather like the American Secret Service men who guard their president.

The young man approached Lady Diana, who had been briefed in her telephone call from Buckingham Palace to expect him. He led her to a green Range Rover parked in a no-waiting area at the side of the airport terminal building.

She sat in the front passenger seat of the luxurious upgraded version of the old well-trusted Jeep-style Land-rover for the drive out westward along the twisting A93 which runs from Aberdeen through the beautiful forest of Glentanar to the River Dee and the purple heather-covered hills surrounding the market town of Ballater and the castle of Balmoral.

With a wave to the policeman sitting guard in the gatehouse entrance to the castle, Diana's driver swept up to the main door of the ancient turreted building.

That night the teen-ager dined with the Queen, Prince Philip, the Queen Mother, and the youngest Prince, Edward, then sixteen years old and still at Gordonstoun School in Scotland, in Balmoral's state dining room hung with stained and torn flags from battle victories long since past. They were served the plain food favored by the Royal Family, roast meat and vegetables with strictly no fattening sauces, by liveried footmen in scarlet jackets carrying silver salvers.

Diana of course knew everyone there and felt completely at ease in the royal company. But her attention was on the Prince, who sat opposite her. Diana had met Charles earlier that summer. Once at Balmoral when she went there to help her sister Jane, married to Robert Fellowes, the Queen's assistant private secretary, with Jane's first baby, and before that at a glittering ball at the Duke of Richmond's Goodwood House during the Goodwood race meeting.

At Goodwood the Prince began to notice for the first time how the shy, vulnerable adolescent had blossomed into full womanhood. He asked her to dance. They waltzed together beautifully but friends took little notice.

In July the Prince discovered Diana's wicked sense of humor, so much like his own, and remembered how she had been part of a large party aboard the Royal Yacht *Britannia* for the Cowes Regatta on the Isle of Wight in the summer of

1979 and how she ducked him in the icy waters of the Solent by tipping over the mast of his wind surfer. There have been few girls who would get away with such impishness. In Balmoral they had laughed again over the prank. It was the laughter they shared which prompted the Prince to suggest to the Queen that Diana would make a fine September guest.

She was not the first young lady to be invited to Balmoral in September. The Davina Sheffield so eagerly sought by the press had been a guest four years before.

The talk was on the salmon leaping in the ten miles of River Dee owned by the Royal Family. Prince Charles suggested an early-morning fishing expedition the next morning and the now not-so-shy Diana was delighted.

She is a fresh and deceptively unsophisticated girl who shares all the delights of the rugged outdoor life favored by the Prince, who had been nicknamed "action man" because of his hunting, shooting, riding, diving, skiing, and racing pastimes. She had been brought up in the country and a day's fishing in icy waters holds no horrors for her.

The next morning after breakfast the couple set off in the green Range Rover with the Prince's favorite gun dog Harvey, a golden Labrador, a set of fishing rods attached to the side of the vehicle in a special rack.

The spot the Prince picked was one of the best fishing spots on the Dee, near a bend in the river five miles from Balmoral where the crystal clear water cascaded over hundreds of small granite rocks. It was a place where he had landed many prize fish and a spot favored by another keen royal angler, his grandmother the Queen Mother. At the grand age of eighty she still came down to these waters to cast her line.

On this overcast, slightly damp, and chilly Saturday morning the couple had the riverbank to themselves. Although one side of the bank was exclusively royal, the other was open to anyone with enough money to afford the pricey fishing permits. There was not even a detective lurking nearby, because the Prince was thought to be perfectly safe inside the thousands of acres of private Balmoral estate.

This was the first time Diana and Charles had ever been completely alone together and what went on or was discussed during the next two hours must forever remain a secret between the two of them. But this is the moment the relationship took off, the moment Prince Charles stopped thinking of Diana as a schoolgirl "full of fun." The discovery of each other, interspersed as always with the laughter from the sense of fun they both share, was the stepping-off point toward love and marriage. Their platonic friendship changed forever from that morning. From that day on the Prince, who always had a roving eye for a pretty girl, had eyes for no one else.

But as they chatted and laughed—the Prince in thigh-high rubber waders out in the current with

Diana sitting on the bank beside a fir tree—the privacy of their two snatched hours away from the world was rudely shattered.

. The Prince suddenly strode back to the bank, an angry look on his face. He reached for a pair of binoculars from the back of the Range Rover and turned them on the opposite bank. Thirty yards across the river a photographer was focusing a long-range lens. It is not clear whether the Prince, wary as a hunted deer over lone cameramen, gave the instruction or whether it was the lady herself who decided with remarkable speed to ruin a scoop for the photographer.

Safely hidden behind the nearest tree, Lady Diana fished in her pocket for a powder compact and using the mirror in its lid she peered furtively out from her hiding place. Photographer Ken Lennox was rewarded with a smudgy print of an angry-looking Prince and the back of a lady in a headscarf peering into her makeup mirror.

On Monday morning the photograph was splashed across the pages of the national newspaper that employed Lennox. It was a look into the future for Diana, a taste of what she must expect, a fate suffered by many pretty girls in the past who have been seen with the Prince. Fleet Street and the rest of the world's press, hungry for romance stories about the bachelor heir to the throne, would never leave her alone now. Her cover was broken before the romance had even started.

The lady moved through the wood, careful to keep her back to the river, and Prince Charles drove on with the Range Rover, picking her up out of sight of the frustrated Lennox, their fishing morning ruined. But the seeds of romance sown that morning in those two stolen hours together would change the lives of both these young people.

That afternoon, with the Queen and Prince Philip, the Prince attended the Highland Games at nearby Braemar dressed in his ceremonial tartan kilt and tweed jacket. There was no sign of the mysterious lady on the riverbank, much to the annoyance of a large posse of reporters and photographers who had learned of the royal game of hide and seek.

On Sunday night Lady Diana was driven back to Dyce Airport but by then her identity had been discovered by the reporters whose interest was sparked off by any lady, let alone a pretty blonde who wanted to play in the woods.

From Heathrow Diana took a taxi back to Coleherne Court and the three flatmates who were desperate to know all about the weekend at Balmoral. A phone call just before midnight pushed the excitement to fever pitch. Prince Charles was calling from his room at Balmoral more than five hundred miles away. He and Diana talked for an hour and a further date was made for later that month when the Prince returned from Scotland.

At eight thirty the next morning she drove a small German car across London to the kindergarten where she had been working, helping to look after fifty infants, four days a week for the last fourteen months. She didn't know it then but it was the last time she would be able to take that twenty-minute drive in peace before the eyes of the world were turned on her.

When she arrived back at her flat at teatime, the first photographer was waiting to snap her; for the next six months there would not be one day when she would be able to return home without finding a cameraman lurking somewhere.

On Tuesday, with the Young England Kindergarten in Pimlico, not far from Victoria Station, under seige by about ten journalists, the lady agreed to pose with two of her charges in the hope, vain as it happened, that they would agree to leave her alone.

But the lady made a slip, or rather forgot her slip, and the ensuing photo session became an incident that left Diana red-faced with embarrassment. The prints that were produced and used in newspapers around the world made Prince Charles, once he had recovered from his shock, roar with laughter.

That Tuesday had begun warm with bright sunshine and Diana had put on a thin cotton gingham skirt bought earlier in the summer from Liberty's, a Regent Street store popular with young ladies of her background. The flowery cotton print looked very cool and fresh. The playground of the Young England Kindergarten behind a church in St. George's Square, Pimlico, was shaded by several flowering cherry trees and the photographers asked her to move out of the shadow to get the sun behind her to enhance her fair skin and blond hair. It is an old camerman's trick to get a sort of halo effect, very flattering in black and white.

Diana walked across the playground with two four-year-old children and picked up one child to pose shyly, standing where the men had asked her. What she didn't realize as the battery-operated motor drives whirred on was that through the lens of their Nikon and Olympus cameras the excited photographers were getting a real eyeful.

The sun shining through the thin cotton dress was to reveal to the world very fine legs and a pair of extremely brief but very fashionable panties. The shots, when they appeared less than two hours later in the first editions of the London evening papers, made the lady blush a deep beet red. "Oh, my God," she exclaimed to the other teachers. "I've never been so embarrassed in all my life."

But the next day when the Prince made his second call to her flat after seeing the same photos in the morning papers, they laughed together as he made jokes about the strong, well-shaped limbs which the world had seen for themselves.

Laughter was an ingredient that had been missing from the Prince's private life for more than two months. The Prince, who admits to being a romantic, falling easily but usually very briefly in love, had been a very lonely young man before the discoveries of the Balmoral weekend. The previous winter he had met another blonde who was to have a profound effect on his life.

Freckle-faced millionaire's daughter, Anna Wallace, was the most independent, outspoken, and fiery girl the Prince had ever met. The slim-waisted, full-breasted twenty-five-year-old woman was also the sexiest of his many conquests.

Their affair began after a chance meeting at a winter weekend hunting party and grew into a passionate and deeply affectionate friendship. Charles became completely besotted with this beautiful woman who was not unexperienced in the ways of men. As a future bride her background was perfect: she had a good pedigree, nothing like the girl who would succeed her of course, but top drawer nonetheless.

Her extremely wealthy father, Hamish Wallace, owned homes and estates in England and Scotland and a house in fashionable Charles Street, Mayfair, just behind the Hilton Hotel. The only thing in her disfavor were a few indiscretions in her past. She had spent three years with two lovers, and that would never do for a future Queen of England.

Charles knew all about the problems of old boyfriends. Davina Sheffield too had a previous lover before the Prince, who had come forward to reveal all to the millions of readers of a popular Sunday newspaper. The revelations greatly embarrassed the Prince of Wales.

But in the winter and spring of 1980 Charles

pursued the lovely Anna, a girl who looked for excitement in life and went braless under silk blouses, a shocking, almost wanton attitude to strike in royal circles.

The Prince invited her to spend weekends with him deep in the English countryside at the homes of several of his trusted friends and made regular late-night visits to her small flat just 'off Sloane Square, Chelsea; ironically this love nest was less than a mile from the flat he would never visit, Diana's home at Coleherne Court.

Fiercely independent Anna, although flattered by the Prince's attentions, was not a girl who would or could easily fall in with the royal lifestyle. She objected to being treated as a piece of baggage, hating the way she had to be picked up by detectives and driven for secret and furtive rendezvous with the Prince. The couple had already rowed over what she considered his chauvinist attitude, although he had tried to explain that their affair could not become common knowledge.

He tried to make their relationship more respectable by showing her off at dinner and private parties, but Anna wasn't satisfied. The wooing of any girl by a prince is bound to be shrouded in secrecy, but Anna wanted none of this. The Prince's friends were getting worried. The two married ladies who had set themselves up as his personal advisers in the love and marriage stakes, Lady Dale Tryon, whom the Prince affectionately calls "Kanga," and Camilla Parker-Bowles, wife of Household Cavalry Officer Andrew Parker-

Bowles, did not like Anna's attitude. From behind the scenes, carefully and cunningly, these
two ladies, once called "the other women in his
life," worked to make certain that Anna would
not be the one. To their minds she was just not
suitable.

Charles believed he was in love with the lovely
Anna and even told one of his male friends that he
wanted to marry her. But before the friends could
move to end the relationship, it was Anna herself
who settled the problem.

She had become sick and tired of her under-
cover life-style and when one night in June at a
ball given by his old friend Lord Vestey the
Prince danced all night with other girls, leaving
Anna alone like a wallflower, her emerald-green
eyes flashed with anger. When finally he did ask
her to dance, the couple rowed and other dancers
heard Anna exclaim, "You've left me alone all
night, now you will have to do without me." She
drove home alone that night and although the
telephone calls kept coming through to her from
Buckingham Palace, she never saw the Prince
again.

Two months later on August 21 in the pages of
The London Times, right next to the official Court
Circular, where Charles couldn't fail to see it, the
very sexy Anna announced her forthcoming
marriage to another man, Johnny, the younger
brother of an English peer, Lord Hesketh. It was
a fine catch and Anna had had her revenge.

Through the months of July and August the
Prince had become a desperately lonely man. He

still carried out his scores of public engagements with style as always, giving no sign of personal unhappiness. But surrounded as he was by his entourage of servants, advisers, and hangers-on, he was still lonely, spending many hours completely by himself in his small apartment inside Buckingham Palace.

But strangely enough during this, the loneliest period of his life, the thought of marriage must have been uppermost in his mind. He might not have a bride but he would have a home.

Suddenly he decided to go house hunting. The management of the Duchy of Cornwall, which is responsible for the thousands of acres of prime land in the lovely green counties of Gloucestershire, Wiltshire, and Devon owned by the Prince as part of his birthright, received an instruction from Buckingham Palace to look out for a suitable large country home with enough style to make it fit for a prince.

A few days later, clutching a glossy full-color brochure from a real estate agent, Prince Charles turned his midnight blue Ford Granada off the A433, through a set of rusting wrought-iron gates, and crunched his way up a half-mile gravel drive. He turned to the man at his side, a representative of Humberts, a firm of upper-class auctioneers. "This looks interesting," said the Prince.

Less than an hour later after wandering through the distinguished Georgian house, its four beautifully appointed reception rooms, nine bedrooms, six bathrooms, and slipping on green rubber boots to tramp around some of the 346 acres of rich arable farmland, the Prince had made up his mind.

"I'll have it," he said simply, and the Highgrove estate in the tiny village of Doughton near the market town of Tetbury in wooded Gloucestershire countryside less than a hundred miles from London became royal property for the princely sum of £800,000.

But before the deal was finally struck, one lady was asked to have her say. Two weeks after their discovery of each other on the banks of the River Dee, the Prince invited Lady Diana to see Highgrove for herself. The Prince wanted a woman's-eye view of what he considered was his dream home..

She would never have even dreamt that one day Highgrove would be the house they would share as man and wife, but perhaps somewhere, even then, the Prince had realized how perfect Diana was for him and needed her opinion of what he considered a rare find in the English countryside.

Diana drove up to the imposing white painted double front door flanked by a fine colonnaded porch to see for herself. Charles was waiting in the magnificent oak-floored main hall beside an impressive marble fireplace. Behind him was a view to the west through a bay window with French doors to the formal garden beyond. Alone together they strolled into the drawing room with its fitted window seats and Irish marble fireplace with a dolphin motif and into the library with its fitted bookshelves to two walls.

From then on the tour of the rooms downstairs seemed endless. The dining room, the billiard room, butler's pantry, kitchen with stone flagged floor and an old-fashioned solid fuel stove. By the lady's standards Highgrove, built in 1763 but later substantially refurbished, is a small house. Her father's huge red brick Elizabethan manor, Althorp, 160 miles farther north near the industrial city of Northampton, was far grander.

Althorp, containing one of the finest private art collections in Europe, was an enormous property, so big that members of the public could be taken on guided tours without any embarrassment or disruption to normal life for the Spencer family living in just one wing. Highgrove would neatly fit into the area covered by staff flats and outbuildings at Althorp. (Pronounced Altrup in the local dialect.)

But Diana was delighted with Highgrove and scampered, giggling, up the wide easy tread staircase into the master bedroom, known at that time by the present owners, Mr. Maurice Macmillan—a Conservative member of Parliament and son of the former prime minister—as the Yellow Room and furnished then with a giant double bed complete with flowery satin-covered headboard.

Then the couple went down the corridor to what could become the most important area of the house—the spot that one day soon may become the focus of world attention. A fully self-contained nursery wing. Lady Diana looked at the nineteen-by-fifteen-foot nursery, itself complete with open fireplace and toy cupboard, before moving on to see the bedrooms meant for a nanny and her maid: two small plainly fitted rooms sharing one bathroom.

The lady was plainly thrilled with Highgrove and later that year after the news of her engagement she would tell her friends: "It's perfect, I just couldn't wish for a nicer house."

II

Their Secret Place

On weekends throughout the autumn and winter she would return again and again to Highgrove, which by then had been stripped of all furniture. The house would become their hideaway from the world.

The Prince adored the house and its beautiful parkland which includes a superbly maintained formal garden dominated by a magnificent cedar of Lebanon. Cut leaf beech and tulip trees are set among the carefully clipped lawns and well-pruned rosebeds.

He had instructed Royal Decorator David Hicks, who had helped design the exotic but tasteful interiors of many royal households, to take a look at Highgrove and submit a basic plan. But he didn't need anybody else to tell him about the reorganization of the stable block, a brick-

and-slate building fifty yards from the main house, which would become home for the Prince's string of polo ponies, his hunters, and his beloved racehorse Allibar, a magnificent eleven-year-old gelding for which he had paid £15,000 the previous year.

Apart from the fact that he adored Highgrove, the house's situation in Gloucestershire held other interests for him. He was always in the area during the winter months, hunting with the Beaufort pack, dressed in his navy and scarlet riding jacket, galloping behind a pack of baying hounds. The Prince of Wales, like many of his ancestors, is never happier than when he is upon a horse and out across ploughed fields and over briar hedges after the scent of a fox.

Royal blood sport activities had caused much controversy in Britain with antihunt groups accusing the Prince and other members of the Royal Family of cruelty to animals. But it was one sport the Prince was determined not to give up.

There was also another reason for buying Highgrove. Just five miles away across woods and a stream lived his sister, Princess Anne; her husband Captain Mark Phillips, a retired army officer turned gentleman farmer and show jumper; and their infant son Peter.

Charles had always been very close to his sister and since they moved from London to live at Gatcombe Park, a country estate not unlike Highgrove, he had been a frequent visitor. Living so close would be very convenient for them both.

During the next few months as the love and

affection grew between Diana and Charles, the clematis, wisteria, and magnolia creeping up the stone walls of Highgrove were beginning to burst into flower. By the end of their honeymoon their new home would be covered with pink, yellow, and blue flowers.

The romance of the century had started but it would be a strange sort of courtship for the twentieth century. The wooing of Lady Diana Spencer would not be all champagne and roses, candlelight suppers or country house parties. There would be tears and subterfuge, despair and loneliness.

The tears would be shed by Lady Diana, overwhelmed more than once by the pressure she faced. The subterfuge and despair would be shared by them both trying to escape the watchers, with prearranged phone calls, long drives, and furtive meetings at the homes of mutual trusted friends.

They would be in love but never be seen in public together throughout their courtship, never hold hands in case anyone was watching. Never relax completely with each other, existing only from one snatched rendezvous to the next.

They would be forced to act as if their relationship were somehow dirty, hiding, forever suspicious, never knowing whom to trust.

The loneliness would be shared by them both: she in her Coleherne Court flat and he in the empty rooms of Highgrove or in his private quarters at Buckingham Palace.

But it was still September, the romance had

only just begun, and their problems hadn't even started yet. Through October the couple met whenever they could with a set arrangement of pretimed phone calls, long late-night drives, and false trails designed to throw off the watching press.

The world had already realized that this wasn't just another of "Charlie's darlings," as the popular press put it. Diana was obviously someone special. Huge in-depth assessments of her began to appear even in the more respectable British newspapers. Diana was being photographed constantly wherever she went by a faithful bunch of cameramen following the scent in the way Charles would follow the hounds. And sensing a winner at last, the men and women journalists from the European magazines which specialize in candid pictures, as well as the North American press, were moving in on the flat at Coleherne Court. A picture of Lady Diana just getting out of her car would get front-page treatment; none of Charles's legion of past girl friends had ever merited such attention.

Diana tried to carry on as usual, dancing with the children who called her "Miss Diana" at the kindergarten four days a week from 9:00 A.M. until 3:30 P.M., and even found time late in the afternoon two days a week to care for a young handicapped child, spending several hours at a flat in exclusive Eaton Square, Belgravia, not far from the kindergarten. The child's name was Patrick and Diana became quite dedicated to him and was upset when the child returned to America with his parents.

As it happened, the kindergarten and her hours with Patrick revealed her love for children. The infants she helped to care for at the kindergarten were only at baby carriage or pushchair age: her work was as a sort of nanny. She may not have realized that she was preparing for marriage and motherhood in a loving and practical way.

Diana's weekends, wherever possible, were spent with the Prince. He was constantly on the phone to her flat, and Carolyn, Virginia, and Ann—who came to be christened the "Trinian belles" after a famous series of British films on hilarious schoolgirl life—were drawn into the royal romance too.

Throughout the six months all three girls were constantly pressured by reporters desperate to get any information on Charles or Diana, but none of the flatmates ever revealed a thing. As Carolyn, who was at school with Lady Diana, said after the news of the engagement, "It wasn't difficult to keep it secret; we never dreamed of telling anyone. We have been very discreet."

Secrecy was the name of the game played by the couple that month, happy in each other's company and determined to try to keep their love from the world as long as possible. Diana was never seen with him in public, although on a number of occasions she had managed to be nearby as he went hunting and shooting. She was in the grandstand at Ludlow racecourse in Shropshire as the Prince mounted on Allibar engaged in his latest hobby, horse racing, the sport of kings. She cheered him and screamed with excitement as he was narrowly beaten into second place. But she sneaked away from the course alone to meet later in the evening to celebrate his near victory over a champagne dinner at the home of one of the Prince's friends.

Long-distance driving around Britain on the network of motorways spreading out from London like a spider's web, all alone at the wheel of her family's small French car, was to become the regular pattern of her life in the months to come as she hurried to another quiet assignation with the Prince. She was becoming used to those long solitary drives.

Even his thirty-second birthday on November 14 had to be celebrated in secrecy. The Prince had gone to another of the Royal Family's country homes, Sandringham, a beautiful but wild and windswept country estate on Britain's cold east coast in the county of Norfolk. The estate was under seige by a small army of newspapermen. Eventually Diana had to say her "happy birthdays" over the telephone and the presents she had bought in Knightsbridge, including two sensible plain white shirts from Harrods, collar size fifteen and a half, had to wait until the press interest had waned. Buying presents for the man who has everything is not easy; neither is being unable to join his birthday party.

In the middle of November came the first taste of the real loneliness and despair she would experience in her new role, and with their first real separation came the first tears.

She had driven down to Highgrove to spend Saturday night, virtually camping out on the now stripped and bare boards looked after only by an elderly Irish couple who had worked for the Macmillans and had stayed on to manage the house for its new owner.

The next morning the Prince had to say his first good-bye of their relationship. That evening he was flying from Heathrow Airport to Delhi at the start of a well-planned royal tour of the Indian subcontinent. For three weeks they would be separated by six thousand miles.

In her flat Diana sat with her flatmates in front of their color TV to watch the Prince's ceremonial arrival at Delhi Airport on the early evening news. On Tuesday night he telephoned her from the palace in the Indian capital which had been the home of the last Englishman to rule India's millions, the late Lord Louis Mountbatten, the man Prince Charles had called "Uncle Dickie." Lord Mountbatten and Charles had planned to take this tour of India and the monarchy of Nepal together, but an Irish Republican Army execution squad had changed all that.

The telephone line from Delhi was terrible—the couple had to shout to make themselves understood—but his call made it obvious that he missed her already. During the next two weeks telephone calls would come in from all parts of India—from Bombay, Madras, Agra, Bangalore, and Calcutta. Sometimes the phone in Coleherne

Court rang in the early hours of the morning. India is five and a half hours ahead of London time and late at night, after an endless round of receptions and dinners, was the only chance the Prince had to get to a phone. Sometimes he took hours to get through; the Indian telephone service is appallingly backward and slow and even the Prince of Wales, an honored guest, did not get much in the way of priority.

It was during one of these bad connections, with the line faltering and breaking up and with a strange echo effect making conversation virtually impossible, that Diana burst into tears.

It was reported she had been bitterly upset by a story in one of Britain's Sunday papers alleging that she had spent an illicit night of love with the Prince before his departure for India, in of all places the carriage of the royal train parked on a railway siding in the West Country. Lady Diana had been nowhere near the train at the time. In fact the night in question she had driven back to her flat after joining the Prince and the rest of the Royal Family at a belated birthday party for Princess Margaret, the Queen's younger sister, in the ballroom of the Ritz Hotel in Piccadilly.

That night had been one of the happiest of their new friendship. Wearing a blue satin gown, her shoulders bare, Diana had danced all night with Charles and had enjoyed supper with her childhood chum Prince Andrew, then twenty, and one of his string of girl friends, a lovely model named

Gemma Curry. Gemma was just nineteen and she and Diana found they had much in common.

The story had ruined Diana's memories of a wonderful fairy-tale evening. And she wept as she told Charles about the innuendo and gossip the story had spread. Her distress upset and angered the Prince, who instructed his private secretary to demand an apology from the newspaper, an unprecedented move for the Royal Family. In any ordinary situation Diana could have sued for libel over such a tale, but the Royal Family had never done such a thing. A court hearing would be unthinkable. In the event the Queen's press secretary, Mr. Michael Shea, wrote to the editor demanding an apology and even issued a copy of his letter to the rest of Fleet Street. Usually the Royal Family ignored wild stories written about their activities; they were all well used to them. Unwittingly, by his anger over Diana's tears, the Prince had revealed how much he cared for her. This chink in his armor did not go unnoticed by the small group of British journalists tailing him on his tour of schools, factories, farms, and ancient temples throughout India.

Amazingly, and most uncharacteristically, the Prince, who over the years had become something of an expert in hiding his private affairs from the press, revealed the first inkling of the strain teen-age Diana had been under since the Balmoral weekend in September. Chatting about nothing in particular to a trio of British reporters at a reception in the British High Commission in

Delhi, the Prince, among all the small talk about the weather and the Indian poverty and way of life, suddenly started talking about the girl they all wanted to know about but didn't dare ask.

"Diana's a very nice girl, you know," he said and quickly added: "All this has been something of a strain for her, you know. At times it has reduced her to tears, but she has coped magnificently."

Then he told about some of the problems and worries running through his own mind about the girl for whom he cared so much. "You must not rush me," he told the amazed men from Fleet Street. "If I get it all wrong you will be the first to criticize me in a few years' time. It's all right for you chaps. You can live with a girl before you marry her, but I can't. I've got to get it right from the word go." It was a rare insight into the secret, very human dilemma that faced the heir to the throne.

The problem facing Charles was, could Diana at the tender age of nineteen, and virtually completely unworldly, be the very special lady who could overcome his doubts, and more? She was obviously a charming, sweet girl, anyone would see that. But did she have enough—to use the words of Queen Victoria talking about Princess Alexandra, the future Princess of Wales, "to take the foremost position in the society of the greatest and richest capital in the world."

Britain, with its soaring inflation and unemployment, was no longer the capital of the world, but the safe and secure British monarchy was at a pinnacle of success. The Crown was popular and much loved. Thousands had turned out that summer to sing "Happy Birthday" to the eighty-year-old Queen Mother. It was a time of great faith in the Queen and Prince Philip, a time when the popularity of the Royal Family had reached a peak.

The problem of whether or not Diana was the right girl bore down heavily on the shoulders of this heir to much responsibility as he finished off an exhausting Indian tour with a trip to the poverty and horror of the most overcrowded city on earth, Calcutta.

The Prince, too well trained to show emotion, came close to tears himself as he walked through the shaded top-floor room at Lower Circular Road, in the heart of teeming Calcutta. Incense smoke drifted across dozens of tiny wooden cots crammed in lines.

He was clearly moved when he saw Leela, a three-day-old girl who had been found barely alive, stuffed like garbage into a dustbin in the filthy slums that cover that vile city.

He had discovered that nothing in the ordinary Western response had equipped him to cope with the shock as Nobel prize winner, Mother Teresa, told him in a quiet matter-of-fact manner that if baby Leela had not been found in time by nuns, the baby would have been eaten by the packs of wild dogs that roam the tin shacks and cardboard shelters, home of countless millions.

Photographers following the Prince had been banned from that upstairs room because Buckingham Palace officials had themselves earlier suffered an embarrassing reaction to Mother Teresa's matter-of-fact statement about life and death.

But two reporters were invited by Mother Teresa to stay behind in the room because, as she pointed out, "Nothing is hidden here. Why should it be?" They watched the reaction in the Prince's face as he peered down at baby Leela, who weighed just three and a half pounds. He put his hand into the cot. The baby gripped his fingers and the tears welled in his eyes.

He turned to one of the reporters. "Wouldn't you like to take her home?" he said. An impossible idea, but it was obvious that he had wanted to find a home for Leela and had dismissed it as totally impractical.

The baby would be discussed with the teenager whose love of children was now common knowledge. Mother Teresa's Calcutta powerhouse of pure love would remain the Prince's strongest memory of India.

He left Lower Circular Road, Calcutta, to pilot his own red Andover of the Queen's Flight a thousand miles deep into the snow-capped Himalayas of the Kingdom of Nepal.

And there, resting after the rigors of the seething caldron of India, Prince Charles found himself alone at last, with time to think.

Later, slightly to the north of Katmandu, Prince Charles finally made up his mind to ask Diana to be his bride. He would not make the actual proposal for two more months, but trekking through the dramatic beauty of the Himalayas had given him precious time to think. He knew that the speculation and excitement would reach a climax the moment he stepped back onto the tarmac at Heathrow.

For three days he walked and camped below the permanent snows of twenty-two-thousand-foot-high Annapurna. He wasn't completely alone, but then these days a Prince never is. But cosseted as he was by security men, porters, guides, and his entourage of secretary, press officer, and personal doctor, the Prince still found solitude, walking out in front on the trails that wound through beautiful green valleys and up into the subtropical foliage of foothills leading to the very roof of the world.

Charles returned to civilization near a small village called Pokhara on December 12. Tanned and unshaven, with a bright red frangipani blossom through the buttonhole of his khaki jacket, the Prince was in a delightfully relaxed mood after nearly four days of living rough in the mountains. Before driving off to a hot bath and a shave to rid himself of the hair on his chin, he said: "It was so wonderfully relaxing, I feel so well. It was marvelous to wake up in the morning, open the tent window, and see the mountains framed like a picture. You could hear absolutely nothing . . . that silence."

Although the trek had been elaborately arranged, it had an authentic flavor with evenings round a campfire, eating freshly caught carp from the lakes. He had even found time for one of his hobbies and had completed two watercolors of mountain views. His Sherpa guide, a strong, short, stocky man called Pertemba, was impressed with the Prince's physical fitness. "He can walk fast," he said. "He was never tired, and always wanted to walk more."

The Prince had obviously enjoyed the chance to get away from the world to think about what was to be the most important decision of his life.

Although one of his trekking party had carried a sophisticated radio telephone, it was used only twice, to inquire about the murder of John Lennon and to ask for one important piece of news for the Prince, the result of the annual university rugby football match between Oxford and Cambridge. The Prince, a Cambridge man, was delighted with the news that his team had won. Apart from those two calls, the Prince had been out of touch with the world for nearly four days.

From Pokhara he flew back to Katmandu and dinner with his old friend, the King of Nepal, in the Royal Palace. His Majesty, King Birendra, is a chubby, bespectacled Old Etonian public schoolboy who is three years older than Prince Charles and regarded by some of his subjects as the reincarnation of a Hindu god. To Charles the King was just an old friend.

The next day he piloted his Andover from Katmandu International Airport three thousand miles to Bahrain with a refueling stop in Oman. It was difficult to fault the conduct of the Prince during the difficult, and sometimes controversial, Indian tour. He had been treated with suspicion when he arrived in Delhi—memories of British colonial rule were still there—but by the end of the tour he had won friends for Britain with his charm, compassion, and diplomacy.

At Bahrain the Prince, accompanied by his Private Secretary Edward Adeane, Press Secretary Warick Hutchings, and a Scotland Yard detective, joined two hundred other passengers on an ordinary British Airways scheduled flight from the Seychelles.

The Lockheed 1011 Tristar touched down at Heathrow late in the evening of December 14. The Prince was home and from the first minute he stepped back on the tarmac, the Prince realized the controversy over Lady Diana was just as strong. A huge posse of newspapermen were waiting.

An excited photographer among the throng accidently crashed into a trash can while backing down a corridor trying to photograph the now clean-shaven and immaculately dressed Prince.

The good humor he had felt, when he stood on top of the world in Nepal vanished with the crash of the trash can hitting the concrete. "Pick it up," he told the red-faced cameraman angrily. "Anyone would think there's a war going on." In an obvious bad mood he strode out to his waiting Ford Granada station wagon. He took the wheel and drove away so fast that he almost stalled the engine. The Prince had received only a temporary reprieve from the controversy raging over his head about Lady Diana, but now he was back in the thick of it.

He could not even get away from it in Buckingham Palace. When he arrived back at his small private apartment straight from Heathrow, he was told the Queen wanted to see him. He could guess what she wanted to talk about.

III

The Prince Makes His Move

The Queen had hardly ever mentioned his previous romances even when the facts were emblazoned across the morning papers. But this time the speculation over Lady Diana had grown to fever pitch and even she wanted to know what was going on. She had told one of the household, "Even I don't know what is happening. He never tells me." She had asked to see him on his return from Nepal because, like any other mother, she was burning with curiosity to know if this was the girl at last.

Her curiosity would have to wait a few more weeks. The next morning Charles was up early—he is by nature an early riser—out of bed most days by 6:00 A.M. at the latest. "I can't see the point in lying in bed, there's too much to do," he once said. He gathered his detective and armed Special Branch backup team and sped off to the West Country to join an early-morning hunt with the Beaufort. He had given his mother the slip and it would not be until Christmas that she would manage to pin him down about his intentions.

From the tender age of twenty-one he had been under pressure from the public, and had suffered very gentle prodding from his own mother and father about the need to find the right girl one day. The older the bachelor Prince, the greater the pressure.

Dutifully he had done all the rounds and met all the right upper-class available young ladies and never really taken to any of them. He had even traveled to Luxembourg, under conditions of great secrecy, a few years previously to meet an available real-life Princess, Marie-Astrid, and discovered that they just didn't have anything in common—especially religion. For Charles the whole idea of an arranged marriage was completely abhorrent. Heirs to the throne of England are not really supposed to reach the mature age of thirty as a bachelor. Even Prince Philip had started telling him, jokingly at first and later after the Prince's thirty-first birthday with much more seriousness: "You'd better hurry up, or there won't be anyone left."

But the Prince had waited. He had always told his friends that he wanted to marry for love and now just a few days from Christmas 1980 he believed he had found it at last. In the next few weeks he would broach the subject of marriage with Diana herself, tentatively at first, without making a formal proposal, because Charles did have one further worry. What if Lady Diana should say no?

He knew that she wouldn't just be making a decision to marry a man; she would be marrying into a way of life, a job, the task of helping Charles with the difficult problem of steering the monarchy into the twenty-first century. He would first hint at the idea of marriage to give her time to think. As he admitted after the news of their eventual engagement was announced, he wanted to give her the chance of telling him, "I can't bear the whole idea." About her acceptance he said, "I am frankly amazed that Diana is prepared to take me on."

It was just before Christmas when Charles and Diana met for their reunion, and he chose the home of his old and well-trusted friends, the Parker-Bowleses, at Allington, a pretty little village near Chippenham, Wiltshire. Diana later told friends that Charles seemed "strangely stifled." But then that was only to be expected from a man who for more than ten years had lived almost the life of a playboy.

His actual words must, of course, remain a secret, but from what had trickled through from Diana via her friends and family, the Prince put it in a sort of "If I were to ask you" way.

He must have been rather taken aback when the lady giggled. She said later that she had immediately felt the absurdity of the situation and couldn't help giggling. The way the proposal was put didn't warrant an answer at that time and the Prince didn't expect one. But immediately, and particularly over the Christmas holiday, wedding plans were discussed.

Diana hadn't said yes yet. But it was still necessary to make plans. A royal wedding requires incredibly complex forward planning. The traditional wedding organizer, the Duke of Norfolk, was asked to keep his engagement diary free from mid-April until July 31. Heads of the Commonwealth and some top government ministers were told that a royal wedding was in the cards, possibly in midsummer.

Christmas separated the couple again. Diana caught a bad case of flu and went to her father's at Althorp for the festivities. Charles spent Christmas Day with the rest of the Royal Family at Windsor and then joined them for their ritual pilgrimage to Sandringham. It had become a tradition for the Royal Family to spend the New Year and most of January at Sandringham, shooting pheasants and riding on the twenty-thousand-acre estate. It had also been a tradition that they were to be left completely alone during this time. In past years the Queen's press secretary had written to Fleet Street editors asking them to respect the royal privacy during their Sandringham holiday.

This New Year the polite request was completely ignored. Hordes of reporters and photographers were dispatched to Norfolk. The year of 1981 began with the Royal Family under virtual siege. As world interest intensified, the crowd of warmly wrapped men camping out in their cars in front of the main gates swelled to fifty at times; the Royals began to lose their tempers. Angry words were exchanged and there was even talk that a royal shotgun had been discharged dangerously close to some of the overeager scribes and spent pellets rattled down on the roofs of their cars.

Lady Diana, who had been invited to join the rest of the Royal Family at this time, had to stay away. Through her press secretary the Queen showed her displeasure. "The Queen is angry at what she considers is an intrusion of her privacy," said her spokesman, who in his spare time writes whodunit Agatha Christie–style thrillers. Prince Charles joined in, wishing a group of clicking photographers a "very happy New Year" and adding, "I hope your editors have a particularly nasty one." Even young Prince Edward showed a bit of schoolboyish bad humor, shouting, "Watch out, you might get shot" to photographers getting a little too close for comfort.

At this a number of Fleet Street editors got cold feet and pulled out their men. Only a couple of the more sensational tabloids kept their men on after the royal outburst.

Before dawn on the bitterly cold morning of January 7, Charles sneaked away from Sandringham unnoticed by the remaining small press posse, who by now had found warm hotel rooms in nearby Kings Lynn. He drove across country to Gloucestershire to meet with Lady Diana at their usual spot, Highgrove. They spent that evening together before a log fire in one of the almost bare reception rooms, and villagers noticed that lights burned into the early hours.

Diana had driven down to Highgrove in her newest acquisition, a bright red brand-new British Leyland Mini Metro. It was rumored, but later denied, that the car, one of the first to be seen on British roads, had been bought for Diana by Prince Charles. But it is significant that the car was purchased from a garage that *does* service and maintain royal vehicles.

It was another early start the next morning; Diana was becoming rather used to being up at the crack of dawn. At 5:30 A.M. the couple drove in convoy fifty miles east along the M4 motorway from Tetbury, he in his Ford Granada with his detective and she following behind in her new Mini. At the Membury service area the Prince took an illegal shortcut through a service road behind the gas pumps and cafeteria, followed by Diana's Mini, and took a back road to the village of Lambourne.

Charles had been in the habit of riding his magnificent racehorse, Allibar, across the Berkshire downs at dawn, training for the next race. He was booked to ride at Chepstow in February. Diana, in thick sweater and green waterproof coat, stood for more than an hour on the edge of the downs watching the Prince put Allibar through his paces. Then a detective drove Diana to breakfast, and after putting his horse back in its stable box and slipping the animal the usual couple of sugar lumps, the Prince borrowed an old bicycle and peddled off to join her.

The couple had been invited to breakfast with the Prince's racehorse trainer, Nick Gaselee. It had become a regular feature of the Prince's cold dawn rides—boiled eggs, toast, and tea to warm him up at 7:00 A.M.

But the fun of breakfast in the Gaselee's kitchen was rudely shattered by the sound of car doors slamming in the quiet lane outside. Diana and Charles had not covered their tracks well enough. Two photographers had driven down from London at dawn just on an off chance when they noticed that Diana's distinctive red car was not parked outside her flat. Now, cameras at the ready, they stood guard outside the white two-hundred-year-old cottage, knowing that Charles and Diana were inside.

Since September Charles had been determined that no one would get a photograph of him with Lady Diana; his determination had become almost something of an obsession. He believed that the press had been responsible for ruining some of his affairs in the past by hounding girls mercilessly and he was not going to let that happen to Lady Diana.

"My, you are up early this morning, gentlemen," he said sarcastically to the two cameramen as they photographed him emerging from the cottage door. He had stayed indoors for fifteen minutes after Lady Diana left to give her a chance to get clean away. Diana had been photographed coming out of the same door but not in the same frame. In fact through clever planning they were never photographed together at any time during their courtship. The first pictures were the official ones on the terrace at the back of Buckingham Palace on the day of the announcement.

But to secure their privacy Diana was to undergo some indignity during the next six weeks. On one occasion she was even forced to lie on the back of a Land-Rover covered by a blanket to escape the cameras. "Not exactly the way to treat a lady," observed the London *Daily Mirror*.

Diana drove back to London and the seclusion of her flat. For the next few days she tried to continue life as normal, kindergarten during the day and suppers with her flatmates before an evening of television. Meanwhile the press were back in force at Sandringham. The Queen had asked Charles to formulate some plan to lure them away.

Charles suggested to Diana, in one of his late-night phone calls, that she should go home to Althorp for the weekend, and in some way drop a hint to the press of her destination. On Friday night Diana drove north up the M1 motorway to Northampton and Althorp. One of the flatmates, who so dutifully guarded their friend, carefully dropped the name *Althorp* to the first of the many journalists who were always on the phone.

On Saturday and Sunday afternoons throughout the winter months from 2:30 P.M. on for the sum of one pound per head, members of the public can go on a guided tour of the splendid Spencer home. Takings were slightly up that Saturday afternoon as pursuing newshounds paid their "quids" to see Lady Diana. They weren't disappointed. She was spotted walking alone through woodland on the estate, warmly wrapped against the cold in a green coat and boots and, incongruously, an old man's trilby hat. "She just wants to be alone," said her stepmother Countess Raine Spencer as she served customers in the Althrop trinket shop. The inference was that the lady was thinking about a marriage proposal; it made good headlines.

In fact that is exactly what Diana was doing. The Prince had made the first move; she knew it wouldn't be long before he popped the actual question.

On Sunday evening Diana drove back home to her flat after her weekend away from it all. One more day of peace and quiet was all she would get before being flung once more headlong into subterfuge and controversy.

Most of the Royal Family, including Charles, were still at Sandringham for the New Year holidays. Diana still had that outstanding invitation from the Queen to join them all for a few days, and the lady was determined to go to Norfolk.

Under cover of darkness she drove east out of London, but cleverly not in her own car. She left her flat in the red Mini Metro but switched, in the grounds of Kensington Palace, where her sister Jane lives, to a borrowed silver Volkswagen Golf.

Diana knew Sandringham like the back of her hand after a childhood spent on a rented home in the Royal Estate. By dinner time she was safely inside dining with the Royal Family.

Two mornings later, in broad daylight, Lady Diana drove straight past the unsuspecting watchers and headed back into London, but not without some help from the rest of the Royal Family.

A neat little plot was hatched to lure the press party away and let Diana escape. Some of the royal males, Prince Philip and Princess Anne's husband Captain Mark Phillips, went off for a pheasant shoot, distracting about a third of the photographers. Meanwhile Prince Charles drove quickly and noisily past the thirty or so reporters and cameramen still clustered round the main gate. They gave chase only to find that he had gone to the dog kennels by a side gate to feed his Labrador Harvey. The Prince smiled knowingly as the photographers had to content themselves with just the Prince. Charles knew that as they wasted film on him, Lady Diana was driving out of a side gate back to London and her flat. She was home by 1:00 P.M.; the press had been beaten again.

The Royal Family met for lunch in a privately booked room at a local public house, aptly named the King's Head. The sound of their laughter could be heard in the saloon bar where the journalists were drowning their sorrows. Even Princess Anne, never one to be helpful to reporters, had earlier wound down her car window to say with a sly smile, "She's gone you know." When Charles finished his pub lunch, there was a gloating tone in his voice when he said: "There is no one here. I wish you would all go away." The crestfallen bunch of newspapermen took him at his word and headed off along the road taken earlier by Lady Diana. There was nothing left for them at Sandringham now. The next confrontation would not be much more successful for them either.

Before Christmas Charles had discussed with Diana the possibility of taking a skiing holiday together. It was a slightly embarrassing invitation for him to make, because three years earlier, while Diana was still a schoolgirl, the Prince had taken her elder red-headed sister, Lady Sarah, to the snows of the Swiss Alps for a ten-day chalet holiday in the jet-set village of Klosters. Now he was inviting Diana to share that same cosy three-bedroom chalet. But Diana, who was a competent skier after a few earlier ski resort holidays with schoolfriends and her family, accepted the Prince's invitation without hesitation. It sounded like a lot of fun.

In the event Charles flew off to Zurich without her on January 23. As the world interest had hotted up, the couple had realized how impractical a normal vacation would become. It would not have looked very proper for the Prince and Lady Diana to be seen coming out of the same small building every morning, especially when the Prince had entertained Diana's sister in the same way just a few years before. Anyway it would have ruined the Prince's determination not to be photographed with her.

For the next ten days the Prince, in a navy ski suit and woolly hat, zoomed up and down the piste, staying in the chalet, which is owned by his old friends Charles Palmer Tomkinson, an ex–British ski champion, and his wife Patti. He took part in a long-distance cross-country race, won a cow bell as a prize, and he phoned Diana every night. He had made up his mind. He would propose marriage to Lady Diana Frances Spencer as soon as he returned to Britain.

IV

Born to Be Queen

The future Queen of England was born in the middle of the hottest afternoon in years. She was a perfectly formed, healthy, bouncing seven-pound baby, but she was not exactly what her parents, Frances and Johnny, wanted. They were both delighted of course with the latest addition to their family, but they already had two daughters and they had lost a baby son tragically. What they had hoped and prayed for was another son, a future heir for the considerable family fortune. On this afternoon, the first day of July 1961, they had not thought of one single girl's name in expectation of a boy.

The new baby took her first public engagement calmly and without tears as she was christened Diana Frances Spencer in a Norfolk parish church. As if in anticipation of her destiny nine-

teen years hence she was born on land and property owned by the British Royal Family—the
large country home, Park House, just a stone's
throw from Sandringham.

With an illustrious lineage that stretched all the
way back to the rule of Charles II in 1630, Diana
was born, like her older sisters Jane and Sarah,
with an automatic title. She was always a Lady by
birth and in the years to come by attitude too.
Diana's family were distantly related to the Royal
Family, and her father, Edward, the eighth Earl of
Spencer, known as Johnny to his family, was
very close friends with the Queen and Prince
Philip. He was also an equerry to the Queen—an
official escort.

Living on the Sandringham estate, Diana virtually grew up with the royal children. There was
just a low dry stone wall separating their homes
and the three princes and their princess sister
would regularly climb over to share the small
open-air swimming pool at Park House. Her regular playmate was Prince Andrew, an angelic-
looking boy two years older than herself; another
playmate was the young Prince Edward.

Looking back now, Diana cannot remember
meeting the much older and, to her as a little girl,
somewhat mysterious Prince Charles. As Diana
grew up at Park House, Charles was away at
preparatory or boarding school. He must have
first seen her when she was still in diapers and he
was a thirteen- or fourteen-year-old schoolboy
heading rapidly for manhood.

She was there, right under his nose, most of his life, but he just didn't notice her. Neither Charles nor Diana can really remember meeting before November 1977, the year of the Queen's Silver Jubilee. The Spencers, their family split by the trauma of divorce, had by then moved to their ancestral home, Althorp in Northamptonshire. It was Diana's older red-haired sister, Sarah, thought at the time to be a flame of the Prince's, who introduced the two as they stood in a muddy ploughed field. Charles had come to Althorp for a day's hunting and he recalled later thinking at the time, "What a very jolly, amusing, and attractive sixteen-year-old." Although he would meet her on a number of other occasions, it would be three years before the courtship really began.

Diana is remembered as a toddler who grew up to be a trouble-free, happy child. Her first governess, Gertrude Allen, now in her seventies, patiently and dutifully read and listened to the infant Diana in the nursery at Park House. "A very conscientious child, she would always try," recalled Miss Allen.

That is how everyone remembers the little girl with the bright blue eyes and the sort of English peaches-and-cream complexion that ladies of other nations would murder for. Diana was always thoughtful, the sort of little girl who was always the first to put a log on the fire, a practical girl who would go around Park House in winter, closing the shutters.

Diana remembers her childhood at Park House

as "a good time of my life." She was too young to remember the unhappiness and heartbreak that split the Spencer family in 1967.

Edward John Spencer's marriage to the fourth Baron Fermoy's daughter Frances in 1954 was the wedding of the year. Diana's mother was only eighteen years old when she walked up the aisle of Westminster Abbey. Almost every member of the Royal Family, led by the Queen and Prince Philip, were there that day. An unlucky thirteen years later, after bearing four children, Sarah then aged twelve, Jane, ten, Diana, 6, and the latest addition Charles, only three years old, Frances decided at the age of thirty-one that she had to find a new life. One day, a servant remembers, Diana's mother "just was not there anymore." She had vanished from the house, leaving behind her husband and children. Her decision created a national scandal at the time, and made the two oldest girls, Sarah and Jane, desperately unhappy.

Only as a teen-ager would Diana be told of the acrimonious divorce in 1969, the arguments over the custody of the children, with family witnesses being called by both sides to testify on their behalf. It split both Frances's family, the Fermoys, and the Spencers right down the middle. Even today Frances, now Mrs. Shand Kydd, will not discuss the bitterness of 1969; the memories are still too painful for her. That same year she married Peter Shand Kydd, whose wealthy family owned a giant wallpaper business.

Inevitably the divorce meant that the four

Spencer children hardly ever saw their mother, but they all adored their father, who had won the court case for their custody. But as Diana grew, so did the emotional links between mother and daughter. Frances's influence was to grow stronger in Diana's adolescent years. Her father lived a solitary life until 1976, when he married the Countess of Dartmouth, the formidable daughter of best-selling romantic novelist Barbara Cartland; but all that and the rather difficult relationship with her new stepmother came at a much more mature period in Diana's life.

The trauma of the divorce came and went relatively unnoticed by the little girl as she moved on to school, first at Riddlesworth Hall, a private preparatory school in Diss, Norfolk, not far from Park House, and then to West Heath, a boarding school in Kent. During her holidays she played with the young royal set from next door by the heated swimming pool. She had become used to meeting the Queen and Prince Philip; she was never in awe of them. To Diana it was rather like meeting her father's bosses: her relaxed attitude in their company would pave the way for the romance of 1980.

Friends say that when Diana first went to West Heath, she had a crush on Prince Andrew. Diana would spend hours gossiping with girl friends about the lineup of the young eligible Royals. In those days the girls, and Diana, had a pet name for Charles. They simply called the Prince "jug ears"; looking at any photograph of the Prince, it is easy to see why.

At West Heath, and later at a Switzerland finishing school, Diana received a typical British middle-class education, but not an intellectual one. Her school friends remember her as a fun-loving, easygoing, and considerate girl, the kind of person who never forgot to send birthday cards on the right day. Her interests were looking after young children, swimming, classical music, ballet, and later skiing, in that order.

A typical school report for the £2,790-a-year West Heath Academy, where Diana studied between 1973 and 1977, would have revealed that she had average marks in English but showed a keen interest in history—understandable with her family background. She had a natural talent for art lessons and was an excellent pupil in the dance classes. Just a few months before her courtship started in earnest, Diana tried to teach Charles how to tap-dance on a concrete terrace at Sandringham; her lesson ended with them both roaring with laughter.

At West Heath she slept with a picture of Prince Charles above her bed. The placing of the photograph was a very strange coincidence, especially in view of the way things turned out. The photograph, of the Prince's investiture as Prince of Wales in 1969, was presented to the school by former British newspaper chief Cecil King, whose granddaughter was a pupil. The picture became a favorite with Diana and the girls who shared her plain white-painted dormitory. The photograph is still hanging in the room to this day.

Headmistress Ruth Rudge remembers that Diana was a delight to have at the school. She was so popular that on her last day she was presented with a cup for special services to the school. "She was always helpful and willing," recalled Miss Rudge. "The dining-room staff liked her a lot because she used to help them with laying tables and clearing up."

A school for the children of wealthy or well-to-do parents, it is set in thirty-two acres of lovely grounds. One of its former pupils was Queen Mary, Charles's great-grandmother. The school's strict timetable gave young Diana a first-class training for later life. West Heath still prides itself on giving girls "a sound general education to train them to develop their own minds and tastes and realize their duties as citizens." Life there was quite Spartan. At 7:30 A.M. sharp the rising bell would ring. Lessons continued until 7:00 P.M. with an extra session on Saturday morning. Lady Diana remembers West Heath as "a thoroughly enjoyable time."

While she was still at boarding school, her father and sisters had left the ten-bedroom Park House for much bigger surroundings at Althorp. In 1975 Edward Spencer inherited the family seat from his father, Jack, becoming the eighth Earl. The stately sixteenth-century house at Althorp is one of Britain's best-kept houses and it contains the cream of the contents of five homes once owned by the Spencer family. The house is filled with pictures by Rubens, Poussin, Van Dyke, Gainsborough, Reynolds, Lely, and many others, all collected by the present earl's predecessors. There are also some fine furniture and extensive collections of porcelain and silver. For Diana, her two older sisters, and her younger brother Charles, it was like moving into a museum. Diana was dividing her holidays between Althorp and her mother's new home on the Scottish island of Seil, where her new stepfather ran a beef farm.

Her relationship with her mother was growing closer and closer. There had been a remarkable similarity between them always. They look very much alike physically, with the same height—five feet ten inches—and build. Both were to become engaged in their teens to glamorous men.

It was during this time of getting used to living in Althorp and flitting between Northampton-shire, her school in Kent, and her mother in Scotland, that the formidable future stepmother entered her life.

Raine Dartmouth's arrival at Althorp sparked off something of a rebellion among the Spencer children. They found it hard to accept her powerful drive and ambition and the huge hold she had over their father. In Raine's mother's romantic novels the groom is always tall, dark, and handsome, and his bride is young, virginal, and dressed in white. There is never any sex in Barbara Cartland's hundreds of paperbacks, just romance.

Raine was like a heroine from one of Barbara Cartland's stories. At the maidenly age of eighteen she had been married to a handsome guards officer, Gerald Legge, who later became the Earl of Dartmouth. Lady Diana's father was at Eton with him.

A slim health fanatic with a porcelain complexion, Raine had boundless energy, every day a whirlwind of activity. At the age of twenty-three she became the London borough of Westminster's youngest councillor and also was famous all over Britain for her welfare work and general do-gooding. In 1976, the year after Edward became Earl of Spencer, Raine suddenly left the man she used to describe as "so steady and strong" and moved into Althorp to be with her husband's old school pal. The Earl of Dartmouth cited Lady Diana's father in the divorce action that followed, but the judge granted a decree because of Raine's "adultery with a man against whom the charge has not been proved."

Two months after the divorce Raine became Countess Spencer. All four Spencer children, including Diana, stayed away from the ceremony, which was a very small affair with just two witnesses. Even Barbara Cartland wasn't invited. Her daughter just rang her after the ceremony to say "Hello, we're married."

The Earl and his new Countess held a celebration party at Althorp a couple of months later and more than one thousand guests attended. But the party could not hide the ill feeling toward Raine, felt throughout the Spencer family and even among the staff at Althorp.

Diana kept away most of this time, but Lady Sarah, never one to keep quiet about anything, made her feelings very clear even before her father married Raine by telling a gossip writer "Lady Dartmouth is an all-too frequent visitor."

Raine told Barbara Cartland, "They won't accept me. Whatever I do is wrong. I just want us to be one close family." To help pay off some of the immense death duties incurred by the death of the seventh Earl of Spencer, Raine went about revamping the house. She sacked some of the old retainers who had been with the family for many years. She opened the house to the public, offering guided tours, and had a souvenir shop built in the stable block, selling trinkets, costume jewelry, and china and even employed staff to open an afternoon tea bar to encourage the day trippers. All this did not go down too well with the Spencer children.

But then near tragedy brought the family together and the children, even Sarah, began to see another side to Raine. She was literally a lifesaver to their father and all the children had cause to thank her.

Just a few days after holding a party celebrating his return to a position of credit at the bank, the Earl collapsed in the stable yard with a massive brain hemorrhage. He was rushed five miles to Northampton Hospital, where doctors told Raine he was unlikely to survive the night. She refused to believe this and immediately chartered a private ambulance to dash seventy miles to a special London brain clinic. She then began a long fight to save his life, swapping doctors and hospitals in her determination. "I wanted to use my life and my energy for his life," she said later. Sitting beside his bed for hours on end, she cajoled and nagged her husband back to life. One day she played him a tape of one of his favorite operas, *Madame Butterfly,* and quite suddenly he just opened his eyes and came out of a long coma. He said later that through his coma he had heard everything that Raine had said to him.

Now there is little evidence of his near brush with death, just a slight blurring of his voice, a little speech hesitation—apart from that he is his usual self. The Spencer girls, who are all devoted to their father, were delighted by what Raine had achieved and relations between them began to improve.

By 1978 Lady Diana, sixteen years old and fresh out of West Heath school, was at the exclusive Institut Alpin Videmanette in Rougemont, Switzerland, a very expensive finishing school for young ladies of wealth and influence. While she was at the school, improving her skiing and learning social poise and grace, her sister was in the same Swiss Alps at Klosters, holidaying with Prince Charles. The holiday was the talk of the press and the school, but Diana never spoke of it. Diana was improving her already good grasp of the French language and her teacher, Madame Barbara Fuls, recalled that "while Diana was a pretty girl, she was not the beauty she's blossomed into now. She knew she wanted to work with children, to get married and have a family of her own, and she once told me that she would only marry for love, not for money or position."

During her brief stay at the Institut, Diana took

domestic science and learned the art of dressmaking and cooking, mainly French or Swiss, certainly not the roast beef of old England.

But she did not last the full course in Switzerland. Suffering from a severe bout of homesickness, she returned to Britain after only two months. Her father decided she should have her freedom and bought her a £100,000 flat, the home she was to have for two years until her engagement to Prince Charles. Diana moved into number 60 Coleherne Court, gathering round her the three girls who were to become her closest friends and confidantes—Virginia, Anne, and Carolyn.

Just like her sisters, Diana had decided that despite her social status she did not want to be a debutante. Becoming a "deb" is the rather strange English ritual involving the introduction of a young woman into London society. It involves an expensive round of parties, dances, and afternoon teas, a tradition with origins deeply involved in snobbery.

Diana wanted none of this; instead of being heralded into society, she slipped quietly into the three-bedroom flat with her three friends. And she took the job she had always wanted, looking after children in a kindergarten.

Her character and her way of life were now well formed and she had grown into a beautiful young woman. She was no longer the slightly rounded giggly schoolgirl Prince Charles remembered, a fact that did not escape him as he watched her stride through the heather of Balmoral. Diana had developed into a fresh, deceptively unsophisticated girl, warm, reliable, quick-witted, open-hearted, and very attractive.

But strangely enough, during this time of freedom in one of the liveliest capitals in the world, Diana never had a steady boyfriend. She went out on occasional dates but they were purely platonic friendships. She never did anything more than hold hands with horsey boys at hunt balls. As her uncle, Lord Fermoy, put it very bluntly, "She has had no lovers."

The only word Diana ever objected to being called was *sweet;* she didn't mind being variously described as shy, innocent, modest, or even quiet, but she did object to the word *sweet*. "I'm a normal person," she would tell reporters. "And I love life."

According to one of her friends, Old Etonian Simon Berry, aged twenty-three, whose parents run a London wine business, Lady Diana broke the hearts of dozens of young men during the two years she lived in Coleherne Court. "Chaps would meet Diana and fall instantly in love," he said. "Many tried to win her, sending flowers and begging for a date, but she always politely declined."

Diana was never one for discos or parties. Occasional meals at her favorite London restaurant, the Poule au Pot in Ebury Street, Victoria, where she would dine with a group, or private dinner parties at the homes of friends were the usual way she spent a night out. She seemed to love cosy evenings in the seclusion of Coleherne

Court with her friends and whatever other friends came to call. Diana chose her friends very carefully, almost as if she were planning for a future in which her past would be closely examined. All her chosen companions were well bred, well educated, and totally trustworthy.

What Diana is instantly remembered for is her tremendous sense of humor. Like Prince Charles, Diana seems to revel in a good practical joke played on her friends, like doing Miss Piggy impressions over the telephone.

During their brief courtship Charles and Diana would roar with laughter together over a brilliant little parody of them in the British satirical magazine *Private Eye*. The *Eye* wrote about their romance in a mushy manner under the byline Silvie Krin. In the regular fortnightly features Diana was always looking at Charles with limpid eyes while he only had evil thoughts on how to deprive her of her virginity. Charles kept all the issues and together they would read them again and again, delighted by the wicked humor.

Like Charles, Diana had acquired a liking for the arts and for music; she plays the piano a little, he the cello. She learned to love driving, passing her test at the age of eighteen. Again like the man she was to marry, she rarely drinks, except for a glass of wine, and she has never smoked.

It was her driving that gave a clue to a hitherto unseen side of Lady Diana Spencer. As soon as she passed her test, she gained a reputation as a demon driver. She was involved in three minor accidents in the first year in which she coped with the pressures of the fierce London traffic. Her first car, a light blue Volkswagen Polo, always seemed to be off the road for repairs to a new dent or scrape, and photographers chasing her at the start of the royal courtship discovered that she enjoyed a good snarl at other drivers who were not quick enough for her as she whipped crisply around central London. One incisive writer described the "reinforcing threads of steel" she occasionally let creep into that well-scrubbed but not over plummy voice when the pressures got a bit too tough.

Strangely enough Diana not only has the Prince's sense of humor, but she also shares a rather nasty habit, nail biting. Both Charles and Diana are secret nail nibblers, a very nervous habit. The Prince always tries to hide his badly bitten nails at receptions and dinner and Diana too coyly tucked her fingertips into the palm of her hand when she showed off her engagement ring to the world.

Apart from this rather odd facet of her character, Lady Diana Frances Spencer had grown up to be a woman with a mind of her own as well as a natural beauty.

Even before her engagement the much photographed Spencer glossy fringe from which she peeped out shyly at the world was being copied in hair stylists' salons all over Britain. Thousands of young girls have adopted her lightly streaked honey-blond hairstyle.

Although she is a very wealthy young lady, Diana's teen-age clothes style was never extrava-

gant. It was not the ususal Gucci, Pucci, and
Fiorucci. She was never caught in anything more
outré than a pair of corduroy culottes, a borrowed
sweat shirt, or a man's corduory smoking jacket.
Her choice of underwear is unknown but she was
once seen perusing the scanty bits of silk in the
upmarket naughty undies emporium in Knightsbridge, run by leading designer Janet Reger.

But she is doomed to a life of flat shoes. High
heels are out for a girl who is as tall as her fiancé.
It wouldn't be protocol to tower over the future
King.

V

Born to Be King

The bridegroom's formal title is His Royal Highness the Prince Charles Philip Arthur George, Prince of Wales and Earl of Chester, Duke of Cornwall and Rothesay, Earl of Carrick and Baron of Renfrew, Lord of the Isles and Great Steward of Scotland, Knight of the Garter.

The Prince of Wales and Earl of Chester are joint titles most closely associated with a male heir apparent of a reigning monarch. They go back to Edward II, who had them conferred on him in February 1301. On the death of a Prince of Wales and Earl of Chester in the lifetime of a sovereign, the titles do not pass on to the current holder's son. They must be re-created with each reign.

Cornwall and the five Scottish titles came by tradition to Charles as eldest son of the sovereign, from the moment the Queen ascended to the throne. Edward III created his son the Duke of Cornwall in March 1337, making it clear that the title should descend to the eldest sons of the kings and queens of England forever.

The Scottish titles go back to the fourteenth century. They were brought to England when James VI of Scotland became James I of England after the death of the first Queen Elizabeth. Charles is now the holder of them as heir to the old kingdom of Scotland.

He was born at Buckingham Palace on the evening of November 14, 1948, and is the forty-fourth heir to the throne. He is also the first male in direct succession in more than eighty years. His ancestors include such unlikely figures as the first President of the United States, George Washington, and the Prophet of Islam, Mohammed.

As Prince of Wales he is in the ancestral line of a pageant of royalty that includes Edward, the classical armor-clad Black Prince of the four-teenth century—who used to feature in so many Hollywood epics starring either Robert Taylor or Tony Curtis; the marriage-prone Henry VIII; and the man who gave his name to both a style of living and an era, Queen Victoria's son, Edward VII. Discovery of his fate came to Charles when he was about eight years old "in the most ghastly inexorable sense." He remembers: "I didn't sud-denly wake up in my pram one day and say 'Yippee'. I think it just dawns on you slowly that people are interested in you and you slowly get the idea that you have a certain duty and responsibility. I think it's better that way, rather than someone suddenly telling you.'' He knows he is one of a dying breed, representing an institution constantly under attack, and that he will be king of a country that has known better days. He has a great faith in Britain, however, and an unfashionable belief in what the country still stands for.

He will inherit one of the oldest crowns in the world. The successor to a monarchy that goes back fifteen hundred years to a Saxon warrior king called Cedric, he is a descendant who commands the greatest universal respect.

In childhood Charles was somewhat shy and introverted, in contrast to Anne, who was ebullient and outgoing. As a toddler he would snuggle up beside his mother on a settee and look quietly at a picture book, or listen to her as she read him a story. The most popular ones were the tales of Beatrix Potter and the adventures of Babar the Elephant and Tin-Tin.

He had enough boyish spirit in him, however, for the Queen, just like any other mother, to have to cope with the pranks and mischief of her son. He raced around the corridors of Buckingham Palace with his friends, played risky games of hide and seek on the roof of Windsor Castle, or slipped pieces of ice down the collar of a footman. When he deserved it, he would get a good spanking, particularly if he was caught being rude to the servants. The Queen took a very stern view of this.

Her Majesty also taught him the value of money, restricting his pocket money to the equivalent of twelve pence a week until he was ten years old, when he was given a rise that made it twenty-five pence. As part of the training for a ceremonial life Charles and Anne were taught to stand motionless for long periods, to accustom them to the duties ahead.

Hundreds of requests came for the young Prince to make public appearances but the Queen resisted them all, no matter how worthy the cause. She remembered how, as a young princess in the war years, she was suddenly thrust into the public arena and she insisted that her son should first of all have a normal childhood, as far as this could be arranged. So the Queen protected Charles and brought him up carefully to the stage when he was gradually made aware of his state duties.

Her Majesty was also determined that her son would not become a palace wastrel, a mere understudy, deprived of any responsibility and forever waiting in the wings. She had seen too much of this in the history of her family. Charles was to be made aware of his future role at the right time, then be prepared for it and given something worthwhile to do in the meantime.

The Queen took special care over the education of the Prince. Sending Charles away to school rather than having the traditional private tuition for him was to set a royal precedent. She decided that, unlike his predecessors, he should go out and meet his future subjects. Her Majesty had been educated behind the railings of Buckingham Palace by a succession of governesses and tutors.

Charles was given the chance to go beyond the royal stockade, and live among ordinary people.

She helped her son through all the usual growing pains of youth and his moments of bewilderment at life. Her encouragement was always there whenever he thought the going was too tough. When he first went away to school, she wrote to him almost daily, feeding him family gossip to keep up his spirits. At university Charles occasionally found the task a struggle and felt lonely. The Queen would visit him privately in his rooms at Trinity College, where they would talk over his problems while he fried a simple meal for the two of them.

The Queen attended to her son's upbringing with a typical mother's gentleness but Prince Philip provided a grittier influence.

The late George V once said: "My father was frightened of his father . . . I was frightened of my father . . . and I'm going to see to it that my children are frightened of me."

Royal paternal attitudes have changed considerably since the beginning of this century, when that palace edict was issued. Charles and Philip have a very close relationship, based not on fear but on love and respect for each other's achievements.

Their personalities differ considerably. Prince Philip has always been the more abrasive, while Charles has more gentleness of spirit. One of the Duke's friends once said: "Charles is not a bit like him."

At first Charles seemed to try hard to emulate

his father. He was tempted to adopt Philip's occasionally high-handed style. But as he grew out of his teens, the Prince developed a likable personality of his own, while his father began to mellow.

They tend to have the same mannerisms: the brisk walk, the habit of clenching their hands behind their backs, and tossing their heads when laughing; Charles too walks around with his left hand thrust casually into his jacket pocket. He has inherited his father's sense of humor; both like zany, outrageous slapstick rather than sharpness of wit.

Otherwise their tastes are usually quite different. Charles adores music, for instance, whereas Prince Philip finds it agonizing to have to sit through a concert. The young Prince can enjoy solitary pastimes, while the Duke is much more gregarious.

Some people close to the family think Princess Anne, Prince Andrew, and Prince Edward take after their father more than the eldest son.

When Charles was a child, Prince Philip did not see much sign of the eventual virile young man in his son. But his father was determined that his son would not have a pampered life. When Charles was a schoolboy, Philip once noticed a servant hurrying to close a door that his son had failed to shut. He shouted: "Leave it alone, man. He's got hands. He can go back and do it himself."

Prince Philip wanted him out of the palace and into the world, rubbing up against other children,

seeing how others lived. He said: ''We want him
to go to school with other boys of his generation
and to learn to live with other children. To absorb
from his childhood the discipline imposed by
education with others.''

He also wanted Charles to pick up a few
bruises and get used to the hard knocks of tough
physical activities. Dancing lessons were stopped,
music lessons cut down, and instead Charles
was sent off to the playing field in Chelsea to get
into the rough and tumble of soccer with other
youngsters. He also went to a private gymnasium
twice a week for gymnastic workouts.

Prince Philip took him out in bitter wintry
weather to teach him to shoot in the mud and
puddles of marshes and over the heather around
Balmoral, where Charles shot his first grouse
when he was ten years old. He taught him how to
fish. Philip is now less keen on fishing than
Charles, who finds the Queen Mother a more
amenable riverside companion.

When Philip was at home, he would spend an
hour after tea teaching his son to swim in the pool
at Buckingham Palace. Charles took to the water
without a hint of nervousness and could swim a
length before he was five years old. Father and
son would have a boisterous game of football in
the palace grounds, with the corgis barking
around their heels. Now and again the Queen and
toddler Anne might join in the fun.

Nearly all his physical skills were taught to
Charles by his father. In this way they grew
closer to each other, and Philip was delighted to

see his son developing into a more self-confident youngster.

But Charles has never had the Duke's ambition to excel at organized games. He still shows little enthusiasm for team games, such as rugby, soccer, and cricket. Individual achievement, where he is testing himself rather than others, has been his forte, hence the generally solitary pursuits he tends to go in for—diving, surfing, flying. His only concession to "team spirit" is polo, which has four men on each side.

Philip introduced Charles to sailing, but he did not develop the same passion for it as his father. The Duke and he rarely go sailing together these days because they do not seem to see eye-to-eye when they are in a boat. Charles explains frankly: "I remember one disastrous day when we were racing and my father was, as usual, shouting. We wound the winch harder and the sail split in half with a sickening crack. Father was not pleased. Not long after that I was banned from the boat after an incident cruising off Scotland. There was no wind and I was amusing myself taking pot-shots at beer cans floating around the boat. The only gust of the day blew the jib in front of my rifle just as I fired. I wasn't invited back on board."

In consultation with the Queen and her advisers, the Duke also influenced the choice of schools for their offspring. He had his way first over the preparatory school Charles went to before moving on to public school. Philip attended Cheam School, which is set in sixty-five acres of grounds on the Berkshire border. It has a history of teaching the aristocracy and the sons of the rich, going back as far as the early seventeenth century. Charles, too, was sent there.

The really decisive part played by the royal father in helping to bring out latent manly qualities in Charles was when the time came to select a senior school for him at the age of fourteen.

Eton, the traditional establishment for top young English gentlemen, was at first favored by the Queen. Charles's name had been put down for a place when he was born. Philip had other ideas. He wanted—and got—his other alma mater: tough, authoritarian Gordonstoun set in a bleak stretch of northern Scotland in Morayshire and based on the principles of German refugee educationalist, Dr. Kurt Hahn.

Gordonstoun had been good enough for the Duke. He thought its harsh, cold-shower regime had done him a world of good, so why should it not do the same for his eldest son? At the time, even Dr. Hahn had his doubts. Charles gave no sign at that age of ever becoming a chip off the old block. Philip persuaded the Queen, however, that Gordonstoun would bring Charles out and make him more self-assertive—in short, toughen him up and smarten him up.

When the young Prince went to the grim institution, he was still shy and withdrawn. Charles remembers now that all the tales he had heard about it made the school seem "pretty gruesome." It was a very nervous young man who was flown by his father up to Morayshire to spend a few bracing years there and, hopefully, end up a man. Philip had reminded him "not to let the side down."

The place was mainly a collection of crude huts. His dormitory had unpainted wooden walls, bare floors, and uncomfortable iron beds. There was the obligatory cold shower to be taken every morning, no matter what the weather. As the school is situated in one of the more exposed and rugged parts of Scotland, the temperature was usually at shivering level. Even the school motto—"Plus Est en Vous" (There Is More in You)—typified a harsh system aimed at stretching to the full both physical and intellectual capabilities.

To bring him down to earth and away from any fancy ideas he might have of being a special sort of fellow from the land of palaces, his housemaster gave Charles a particularly humiliating daily task in his first term—emptying the garbage cans. Dr. Hahn described the school and his methods as one where "the sons of the powerful can be emancipated from the prison of privilege."

Charles may have been reluctant to submit to the rigors of Gordonstoun, but he never quarreled with his father's decision. He hated the school at first, became terribly homesick and did not fit easily into the regime. After four years Charles ended up liking the place, just as his father had done. He became head boy and, shrugging his shoulders, pointed out that it was not really as tough as he had expected it to be.

He excelled in geography and modern languages, captained the school's cricket and hockey teams, and represented Gordonstoun in interschool athletic meetings. He also took the title role in a production of *Macbeth*.

A few years after leaving Gordonstoun, though, he said: "I did not enjoy school as much as I might have, but that was because I am happier at home than anywhere else."

Charles once spoke of his father's influence on his education: "His attitude was very simple. He told me the pros and cons. Out of all the possibilities and attractions he told me what he thought best. Because I had come to see how wise he was, by the time I had to be educated I had perfect confidence in my father's judgment. When children are young, you have to decide for them. How can they decide for themselves?"

He has a fascination for history which he carried with him from Gordonstoun to Trinity College, Cambridge, where he studied archaeology and anthropology during his first year. He had an average Class II, Division I, pass in his tripos on these subjects before switching to modern history for his last two years at the university, at the end of which he took a Bachelor of Arts Honours degree. "When you meet as many people as I do," he said, "you become curious about what makes men tick and what makes men tick differently."

His exam papers are preserved for posterity in the royal library at Windsor. His tutor on social anthropology commented in a supervision report: "He writes useful and thoughtful essays, although sometimes they are a little rushed. He is interested in discussion—likes to draw parallels between the peoples we study and ourselves.''

At Cambridge he developed a love for the stage and knockabout farce. He appeared in undergraduate revues and earned himself the nickname Clown Prince.

He has links with Australia that go back to his schooldays, when he spent a year at Timbertops—the abrasive, open-air school in the mountains north of Melbourne. He has returned to Australia regularly ever since. With his love of risking his neck now and again, he goes down well with a people who like a bloke to prove his courage.

He regards the year he spent at school in Australia as "the most wonderful period" in his life. The Australians responded to his affection for their country and themselves with such endearing terms as "Good on yer, Pommy bastard." Part of his transition from nervous teen-ager to confident man took place there; away from the protecting arms of his family he learned to stand alone.

It was Australia that opened his eyes: "You are judged there on how people see you and feel about you. There are no assumptions. Having a title and being a member of the upper classes as often as not militates against you. In Australia you certainly have to fend for yourself." He grew to love the rough-tongued, tell-it-to-yer-straight Aussie character. He liked the muscular and dynamic life.

The Prince's liking for swimming fits in perfectly with Australia's beachside way of life. When he paid an official visit in 1974, he spent as much time as possible in the sometimes treacherous, rolling seas.

At Coolangatta he watched local beach rescue squads in operation in the risky surf. He persuaded the beach guards and anxious local officials to allow him to ride in a powerful new rescue craft. Once in the boat he took over the controls himself, and flew across the waves.

During that tour of Australia and New Zealand he rolled up his sleeves and joined the sheep shearers. These men, who earn their living clipping wool to clothe most of the world's backs, are among the toughest and roughest workers anywhere. Holding hundreds of struggling sheep between your legs every day, and having to reach a seemingly impossible target to earn a decent living, makes the shearers men of hard sinew and muscle. Charles took to them immediately, and they to him, when he called at a sheep station near Wellington, New Zealand. Their way of life interested him. He asked them about their homes, their families, and what they wanted in the future.

Then the "gaffer" of the shearers asked Charles to lend a hand. A dozen or so bewildered beasts were brought up and HRH swung into action with a pole, pushing the sheep through a murky, foul-smelling dip. It was a bit of a struggle and he doubted whether he could ever have earned a week's wages on the job. But he learned a little more about one tiny part of his future dominion.

Abroad, especially in the Commonwealth countries, his stock with everyone from New Zealand sheep farmers to Fijian dancing girls seems to rise every year. He is particularly welcome in Australia, where he has been given the supreme local tribute of being called a "ruddy decent Pommy," an accolade that Aussies bestow on few Englishmen!

The Queen made Charles a Knight of the Garter, one of the oldest orders of chivalry in the world, when he was ten years old, but he was not invested and installed in the Royal Chapel at Windsor until 1968, when he reached the age of twenty.

One of his first formal steps toward the eventual responsibility of the throne was in the autumn of 1972 when, at the age of twenty-three, he was appointed a Councillor of State—together with the Queen Mother—to handle the official affairs of the realm while the Queen visited Australia. This function is vital to the running of Britain and the Commonwealth because, constitutionally, the works of governments at home and abroad have to be officially approved by the Sovereign or her properly appointed representatives.

Charles embarked on his first solo royal tour soon after he came down from Cambridge in 1970 when he went off on a twenty-five-thousand-mile round trip to Fiji and New Zealand. This seemed to set the pattern for all his future public appearances. He asked for as much informality as possible, taking the wind out of official stuffiness.

Charles's interest in the social conditions of modern life, his awareness of community problems, and concern for the well-being of the nation have been demonstrated in his work for Wales.

When the Queen and Prince Philip decided the time had come for Charles to take up the title of Prince of Wales, they were determined that, unlike the late Duke of Windsor when he had the role, their son was to develop more than just a nodding acquaintance with the place. He was to learn the Welsh language and culture and the history of the principality.

His involvement in all things Welsh now includes being Colonel of the Welsh Guards, the youngest regiment of the Brigade of Guards. It is in their uniform that he rides with his mother every June to take part in that most spectacular ceremony of Trooping the Colour, on Horse Guards Parade in London.

He first donned the white-plumed bearskin and scarlet jacket for this celebration of the Sovereign's birthday while he was in the Royal Navy in 1975. Since then, and for the future, it has become one of the most important yearly engagements in his diary.

This mounting involvement in public events has taken the heir closer to millions on a global scale. He feels nothing is too much trouble if it helps him to establish a link with those he will rule.

VI

Those Spencer Girls

Lady Diana Spencer has no past, no previous lovers to suddenly emerge from the woodwork with lusty tales for the scandal sheets. Her pedigree and her morals make the perfect royal bride.

There is nothing in her background to compare with what one Spencer girl got up to with the then Prince of Wales two hundred years ago, back in one of the branches of Diana's complex but impeccably noble family tree.

Georgiana Spencer's naughty nights were the scandal of the nation in the late eighteenth century, and her sister Henrietta's bedtime activities were pretty hectic too. Both girls were the daughters of the first Earl of Spencer, Diana's great-great-great-grandfather. The sexy Georgiana was married at the tender age of seventeen to the Duke of Devonshire, a dry, lifeless man whom she was soon calling "the dog." Bored by her life-style, Georgiana began taking lovers, and her games between the sheets soon became the talk of society gossips.

She briefly became the mistress of the Prince of Wales, the amorous fun-loving playboy who became the grotesquely fat Prince Regent and later King George IV. The passionate prose in the letters she sent the Prince at the peak of their affair in 1785 would today be described as pornography. The letters delighted the Prince, who carefully locked them away. Unfortunately for modern historians, 130 years later King George V was so shocked when he read Georgiana's hot words that he ordered the letters to be burned.

The Prince believed that he was the father of Georgiana's love child born in 1785, but in fact any one of a number of other lovers, and even Georgiana's husband, could have been. Among her many lovers was Charles James Fox, a great politician of his day who supported the idea of American independence. Georgiana believed she was in love with Fox and even tried to leave her husband, the dry Duke, for him. But then she became infatuated with a new man who had entered her life, a future British prime minister, Charles Grey. At the time Georgiana seduced the twenty-one-year-old Grey, she was twenty-eight. In 1791 she became pregnant again but this time she could identify the father: it was Grey. This time even the boring old Duke became angry over his wife's antics and was threatening to throw her out.

She left for the south of France to have the baby there to avoid further scandal. The child, a girl, was eventually brought up in Grey's Northumberland home. In 1793 Georgiana went back to live with "the dog" but continued with her menage à trois, even taking a new lover to add to her collection, the Duke of Bedford. Today a stunning painting of Georgiana as a child by Thomas Gainsborough hangs in the Marlborough Room at Althorp. Gainsborough called it "the face without a frown."

Georgiana's sister, Henrietta, who became Lady Bessborough, was also a busy girl, but not to quite the same extent as Georgiana. The Prince of Wales offered to make Henrietta his mistress too. She refused. She kept most of her love life secret but found in her diary after her death was the following little note. "I must put down what I dare tell nobody, in my 51st year I am courted, followed, flattered, and made love to, *en toutes les formes*, by four men." Those early Spencer girls were totally outrageous, but they weren't the only dark secrets in Diana's ancestry.

Like many British aristocrats, Lady Diana is descended from men and women who were born on the wrong side of the royal blanket. Her links go all the way back to the womanizing King Charles II (1630–1685), who had countless notorious wild love affairs, producing many illegitimate children. Five of Diana's forebears were bastard children of Charles II. Mr. Patrick Montague Smith, a director of *Debrett*, the *Who's Who* guide to the British upper class, said, "The Spencer family, like so many others today, are descended from those children."

There was once another Lady Diana Spencer, too, who almost became Princess of Wales. There were rumors in 1729 that this Lady Diana might marry into the Royal Family. The Duchess of Marlborough tried to engineer Diana's marriage to Frederick, Prince of Wales, a son of the Hanoverian King George II. But instead she married the Duke of Bedford and Prince Frederick married a German princess.

The Spencer family, which traces its links back to the French followers of William the Conqueror, has been in public life since the fifteenth century. Members of the Spencers have been politicians, diplomats, soldiers, merchants, and naval officers. The family motto, "God Defend the Right," gained its first title in the beginning of the sixteenth century when sheep farmer John Spencer was knighted by Henry VIII. Another John Spencer was made the first Earl of Spencer in 1765.

There is an intricate link between the Spencers and the Royal Family. The two families have a common ancestry dating back through Richard II in the knightly, bold fourteenth century; Henry VII, the first Tudor king, who encouraged John Cabot to sail to North America in the fifteenth century; and James II, who was also for a brief three years King James VII of Scotland in the seventeenth century.

The links make Lady Diana a seventh cousin once removed of Prince Charles. But they are quite far apart enough for them to marry. Lady Diana's connections through blood run on and on. Enterprising genealogists have already linked her, through an American branch of the family, to seven U.S. presidents, including John Adams and Franklin D. Roosevelt.

The Spencers are part of England's real aristocracy, the upper class of wealth and position that existed before the Industrial Revolution, when lots of people who owned factories were given titles. There are only about 150 families that fall in this category.

Mr. Harold Brooks-Baker, expert on the English artistocracy and managing director of *Debrett's Peerage,* insists that despite their pedigree breeding the Spencers are a relatively dull bunch. "There is nobody in Lady Diana's family of any great importance," said Mr. Brooks-Baker. "They are nice people who live in beautiful houses and have the good fortune to be related to almost every member of the aristocracy."

That is exactly the right kind of background for the girl who was born to be Queen.

VII

Charlie's Girls

Lady Diana, like the rest of the world, has known about his reputation as a ladies' man. After all, even her own elder sister, Lady Sarah, was one of the Charlie Set—or Charlie's Angels, as some people called them—for two years.

And it was through Lady Sarah, now married to a businessman, that Charles first met Diana. But Charles barely noticed her: he was more interested in Lady Sarah.

Charles's string of polo ponies could never match his string of girl friends. They ranged from his first love, while he was at Cambridge University as an eighteen-year-old, the stunning dark-haired and fiery Chilean Lucia Santa Cruz, to the sexy blond British actress Susan George, one of the latest Charlie Girls before the engagement.

Over the years he had girl friends in many parts

of the world, most of whom remained friends and kept happy memories of their relationships—even after they went off and married other men.

They were usually fair-haired or blond—and sexy. Most of them said after they were dropped for yet another new face, "Charles was very romantic. He always made you feel that you were the only woman in the world."

Throughout his many years of discreet meetings in the country, on desert islands, or quietly in his apartments at Buckingham Palace, Charles had the pick of the best. Yet he never fell in love, apart from Anna Wallace, with whom he was besotted.

While Prince Charles was at last showing off to the world his bride in the garden at the back of Buckingham Palace on their engagement day, the Band of the Coldstream Guards marched to the front playing "Now Your Philandering Days Are Over."

This song from *The Marriage of Figaro* seemed very appropriate, because one thing is for certain—Charles is going to have to change his life-style after the royal wedding.

Having a string of girl friends would not be unusual for any other eligible bachelor, but with Charles every one of them was brought into the national queen-spotting game. He admitted that occasionally he would look at one of his regular companions and ask himself: "I wonder if I could ever marry her?"

The Prince had always said that he would get married when he was "around thirty" and he had very down-to-earth views about committing himself. His marriage had to be for keeps, without any question of subsequent divorce. He regarded it as a frightening decision because of the special need, in his case, to find the right partner to live with in harmony. "I hope I will be as lucky as my own parents, who have been so happy," he once said.

He told an interviewer: 'Marriage is a much more important business than falling in love. I think it is essentially a question of mutual love and respect for each other. Creating a secure family unit in which to bring up children and give them a happy, secure upbringing, that is what marriage is all about—creating a home."

When he cast his eyes around the world's palaces, he had precious little to choose from. There was a dearth of princesses waiting in their ivory towers for Charles to come whirling in by helicopter and whisk them away. There were hardly any in the same age group or with the same interests as the British prince.

A few tentative steps were taken by Prince Rainier and Princess Grace of Monaco to push forward Princess Caroline as a suitable partner a few years ago, but this came to nothing. When Charles met Caroline at the Variety Club gala in Monte Carlo in the early summer of 1977, he jested: "I've only met the girl once and they are trying to marry us off." They waterskied, dined in some of the world's most elegant salons, and generally tasted the delights of the Côte d'Azur, but eventually it became clear that nuptials were not what they or their families had in mind. The beautiful Princess returned to her sophisticated life among the stylish "Tout Paris"—and an ill-fated marriage—while the Prince flew away to London to the more mundane job of helping to organize his mother's Silver Jubilee celebrations.

There was always wide-spread speculation about Prince Charles and his girl friends. The teen-ager who tended to look like a plum pudding grew up into an attractive man. He was an elegant and eligible bachelor with a disarming smile, easy gentle manner, and a friendly glint in his eyes. He was seen with many lovely ladies but special dates usually escaped the gossip columns.

He was particularly discreet with anyone he really cared about and meetings took place well off the beaten track, sometimes in a trustworthy friend's house. He has a private retreat in the Scilly Isles, for example, where he can relax away from the public eye.

One of his first romantic liaisons occurred when he met Lucia Santa Cruz, the stunning daughter of a former Chilean ambassador in Britain. Latin in temperament, very beautiful and feminine, but a clever historian with degrees from both London and Oxford universities, she was then the chief researcher at Cambridge, working on the memoirs of British statesman, Lord Butler.

Charles was completely fascinated by her for a time, but their friendship died. His family did not look with great enthusiasm on the young Prince becoming too deeply involved with a woman four years older than himself, and a foreigner to boot. Their romance ended, but she was one of the most significant women in his life.

According to friends from that university period, Charles "discovered" girls at Cambridge.

When he began to build up his "string" of international lovelies, he sometimes went to great lengths to be seen with fun-loving girls who were willing to be decoys, drawing attention away from the girls who really featured in his life.

The American admiral's daughter, Laura Jo Watkins, who was briefly seen around with the Prince in 1974, was, according to some of his friends, brought on the scene to take the heat off that year's romance with Lady Jane Wellesley, daughter of the Duke of Wellington. Blond and college-girl pretty, Laura Jo did not mind. She told the folks back home, "I had a fantastic time."

He never hid his clear appreciation of women. During a tour of Fiji, as he was about to depart from a village in a Land-Rover, an outstandingly beautiful dancer, clad only in a bikini top and grass skirt, beckoned to him. Although he was surrounded by the usual entourage of officials and watched by hundreds of people, he walked over to the girl, who draped a garland around his neck and kissed him. He put his hands on her waist and returned her embrace. He kissed her again and from the happy look on his face he obviously enjoyed the encounter. There have been some regal advisers at Buckingham Palace who disapproved of a future king embracing a South Seas dancing girl, but their views were unlikely to influence Charles.

Later that year Charles returned to Fiji. He was guest of honor at the tables of various chiefs in this carefree, natural corner of the Commonwealth. At one function the local chief put two pretty girls on either side of the Prince, changing them every half hour throughout dinner so the royal bachelor would not become bored.

Some of the attractive native women dancers held out their hands and begged Charles to dance with them. Wearing a multicolored shirt and a garland of flowers, he moved onto the dance floor a little gingerly. His dancing companions, with mischievous looks on their faces and gyrating midriffs, moved faster to the music of the drums.

They danced a complicated local pattern, but the Prince soon got the hang of it and seemed to enjoy joining in the fun. One partner was an especially beautiful girl with a hint of naughtiness in her eyes and movements. It was only afterward that he realized why. She had trapped him into a traditional island love dance.

During one official Pacific tour he just took off with a girl to a small, deserted, palm-tree covered island. His blond partner was Jeanette Stinson, the twenty-three-year-old daughter of Fiji's minister of finance, Charles Stinson. They sneaked off to the remote island of Vomo, where they walked across the white sand together, played around in the surf, and sunbathed under the blazing sun. Jeanette had first met Charles two years earlier when he visited the area in H.M.S. *Jupiter*. She said later: "We are friends but it would be wrong to call me a girl friend."

When Princess Anne became betrothed to Captain Mark Phillips, a commoner, it brought Charles a double joy. One was because of the natural love he has for his sister, but the other pleasure came from the fact that his new brother-in-law did not come from the international Royals. The acceptance of a commoner by the Royal Family, the government, and the people of Britain and the Commonwealth widened the choice available to Charles. He could decide on someone who had not been born to the sound of saluting guns.

Any girl from the ranks would still have to be from a good family, however, well educated, and have an unshakable sense of duty. Knowing his taste in girls, she would also have to be a good horsewoman, an excellent swimmer, enjoy an outdoor life, have an interest in music and a taste for adventure, and share his sense of humor. She did not have to be a classic beauty. She needed to be attractive and presentable more than an absolute stunner. Her clothes would be in delicate good taste, not flamboyant, although he has never been noted for his awareness of what a girl friend is wearing.

These qualities were what attracted the Prince to the blond and lovely Davina Sheffield, the ex-debutante daughter of an army major. Davina and Charles first became involved with each other when Davina spent part of her summer holiday with the Royal Family at Balmoral. But four months later they broke up.

Davina rather dramatically left London and headed for Vietnam, offering her services to international relief organizations. Because she had no nursing or medical training, she could not get the sort of work she wanted to do among the sick and wounded. She did, however, find something worthwhile to do. She looked after sixty abandoned or orphaned youngsters in a rundown Saigon house. It was tough going, in miserable surroundings.

When the Viet Cong began to take over the country and infiltrate into the southern capital, she hung on for as long as possible before fleeing to Thailand just days before the Communist takeover. She told friends in Saigon who were trying to persuade her to leave before it was too late: "I feel a real sense of purpose here and don't want to leave."

From Bangkok she went to Australia for a short while before returning to England and another meeting with Charles. Their mutual friends were delighted to see the two of them together again. He gave formal acknowledgment of his feelings for her by producing Davina in public once more as his glamorous and laughing companion during polo at Smith's Lawn, Windsor.

During that long summer they spent more and more time together. Whenever he could get ashore from his naval duties, he would be with Davina at some quiet country retreat, dining with just a few close friends, or having her meet his family again.

Occasionally they would speed away in his 140 mph Aston Martin Volante to what was once a secluded beach for surfing at Bantham, near Kingsbridge, Devon. This seclusion ended when Davina was caught in the nude in the men's changing room. She did not bat an eyelid when confronted by the local beach guard, but word spread around about the couple's visits to the place and one more secret trysting place had to be crossed off their list.

For three months in 1976, while Charles was mostly at sea skippering a minesweeper, they did not see each other. But by September they were hand-in-hand again.

Davina came from landed gentry stock and was a cousin of Lord McGowan, one of the newer baronetcies. Vivacious, intelligent, warm, and sensitive, with a ready wit, she was a suitably well-brought-up young "gel," fit for an English prince.

Apart from the terrible scenes she witnessed in Southeast Asia, she also knew tragedy in her own life. Her widowed sixty-two-year-old mother was murdered, battered to death, early in 1976 at the family mansion at Ramsden in Oxfordshire.

Prince Charles's natural sympathy for anyone in distress was a great help to her during the months she tried to get over her grief. But revela-

tions about her past from an old boyfriend in a
British Sunday newspaper blighted her chances
of marriage to a prince.

Some of his girl friends meant a great deal to
the Prince, but many were fleeting fancies. Few
of those young ladies who claimed they had
something special going for them with the heir
apparent, or who were gossiped about, really did
have close romantic ties with him. But there have
been others besides Davina whose friendship
Charles valued greatly.

There was a long line of suitable young ladies,
all of whom had impeccable pedigrees. Among
them were Lady Henrietta Fitzroy, eldest
daughter of the Duke of Grafton, whose mother
was Mistress of the Robes to the Queen; Lady
Charlotte Manners, model-girl daughter of the
Duke of Rutland; fellow crazy-humor lover
Angela Nevill, whose parents Lord and Lady
Rupert Nevill were close friends of the Queen;
flaxen-haired Bettina Lindsay, offspring of a Tory
politician, Lord Balniel, and who favored a beat-
nik life-style; a onetime firm favorite, Georgina
Russell, the elegantly beautiful daughter of
British diplomat Sir John Russell; and of course,
Lady Jane Wellesley.

For more than two years the pretty and petite
only daughter of the most noble of families, the
Duke and Duchess of Wellington, reigned supreme as the closest female companion of the
Prince. They seemed so complete. She was always there waiting when he returned from the

sea. Then, inexplicably, she suddenly faded from public view for about two years.

During the summer of 1977, however, Lady Jane Wellesley and Charles became close friends again, reviving speculation that she might become a royal bride.

His friendship with Lady Jane cooled off and Charles turned, among others, to twenty-six-year-old Caroline Longman, daughter of wealthy publisher Mark Longman. She was strikingly similar in appearance to Lady Jane and became a regular dinner and waterskiing companion. Her mother, Lady Elizabeth Longman, was a bridesmaid at the Queen's wedding in 1947.

Another frequent companion at this time was Fiona Watson, the beautiful daughter of Yorkshire landowner Lord Manton. She had a slightly more flamboyant side to her character, having once filled eleven pages of *Penthouse* magazine with pinup pictures of herself. These are not quite the qualifications for future queenhood, but Charles found her fun to be with.

He had always insisted that he would not get married until he was around thirty, "after one has seen a great deal of life, met a large number of girls, fallen in love now and then, and one knows what it's all about."

His sound, sane approach to love was always worthy of inclusion in a marriage-guidance pamphlet: "I feel an awful lot of people have got the wrong idea about what love is all about. I think it is more than just a rather romantic, glamorous idea about falling madly in love with somebody and having a love affair for the rest of your married life.

"I think it's much more than that. It's basically a very strong friendship. As often as not you have shared interests and ideas in common and also have a great deal of affection. I think where you are a very lucky person is when you find the person attractive in the physical *and* the mental sense.

"In many cases one falls madly in 'love' with somebody with whom you are in fact infatuated rather than in love. To me marriage, which may be for fifty years, seems to be one of the biggest and most responsible steps to be taken in one's life."

With his engagement to Lady Diana, Charles is going to have to put away what must be one of the most enviable address books in the world. Over the last few years there had been a long glittering list of contenders for his heart. Prince Charles had been doing plenty of wooing . . . but he didn't win them all.

His last girl friend before Lady Diana, wealthy Anna Wallace, turned him down, and friends insist the relationship ended on a stormy note. The blond ex-debutante had almost all the right qualifications—elegance, a good background, and a love of sport. But she also had that past involving other lovers—and a fierce sense of independence. His attempts at reconciliation were to no avail.

It was always almost certain that Charles would marry a Protestant, or someone willing to become one.

Lady Diana, a descendant of a long line of Protestants, fitted the bill perfectly. She would cause none of the fuss and bother of some of the foreign, but Roman Catholic, princesses Charles's name had been linked with.

Apart from Grace Kelly's daughter, Princess Caroline of Monaco, other European princesses lined up as potential brides included Princess Nora of Liechtenstein and Princess Katarina of Yugoslavia, who have still to find their own Prince Charming, and Princess Marie-Astrid of Luxembourg who eventually became engaged to a German count.

But suitable princesses were always very thin on the ground. There was always an abundance of candidates, as he happily found, in the smart town houses of Belgravia and affluent halls in the shires. Because of this it always seemed likely that he would marry a girl from a noble British family.

So there were many fine-bred English mamas who once hoped their daughters might be the bride, who were shattered by the news of the Prince's final choice. Extra glasses of consoling sherry were certainly called for in many fine country homes and mansions on that day!

Close friends or just passing fancies, most of his women have happy memories of the Prince. They say he was an attentive, amusing escort, who had the delightful knack of making the woman with him feel she was the only other creature in the world at that moment.

Throughout fourteen years of meeting girls, from being a shy meek sort of student—the sort of man a Charles Atlas bully would kick sand on—to the virile muscular fellow he is today, Charles never fell in love with the right woman. As the years went by, he became more sophisticated in his treatment of women. A very experienced man-of-the-world indeed. But never the love both he, his family, and, very important, the nation would agree upon.

These must have been very confusing as well as exciting years of romance for Charles. He allowed a glimpse of his bewilderment with his life as the great eligible bachelor at the time he was questioned about love on the day of the engagement to Diana. He answered, awkwardly: "What is love? Whatever love means you can put your own interpretation."

What love means to Lady Diana is that she expects him to take only her to his hideaway on the Scilly Isles from now on, and also that he disposes of a £100,000 house he kept two miles away from Buckingham Palace in Kensington for the odd secret engagement with girl friends.

Lady Diana was among those he invited for intimate dinners at this house in Campden Hill near London's Hyde Park not far from Princess Margaret's home. The existence of the hideaway in this area of expensive and fashionable early-nineteenth-century streets was a well-kept secret, even within the Royal Family. Only a few members of Charles's most trusted circle knew of it. The house was bought for the Prince's use at the beginning of 1980, and it was here that he conducted most of his courtship of Lady Diana.

It was certainly a perfect address as far as Lady Diana was concerned. Her eldest sister, Lady Jane Fellowes, lived just minutes away. Nothing was simpler for Lady Diana than to slip unnoticed up the road to the Prince's haven.

Charles used to turn up in the darkness, without any of the usual fuss and bother about security details and official cars. It was a perfect bachelor hideaway, where his comings and goings went on unnoticed by the neighbors. There were occasions, however, when he had to wait in a car out of sight until a neighbor taking a dog for a walk passed by. The very secrecy of the address added spice to the relationship between the two, as they dined and held hands together in the room decorated in Regency style.

The nearest pub was called, ironically, The Windsor Castle.

No one ever discovered this, or other secret trysting places in cottages through Britain that Charles would speed off to in his Aston Martin sports car or by helicopter with that glamorous string of girls.

As one of his guests in the recent past, Lady Di knows all about them, so she is said to be keeping a close eye on how all the trappings of his bachelor past will be disposed of.

Diana also brought up the subject of two

women who have been closest to Charles for at least five years . . . both the wives of two of his closest men friends.

In London his favorite hostess had always been bubbly blond Lady Dale Tryon, the twenty-nine-year-old wife of banker Lord Anthony Tryon. She was often hostess for dinner parties at the Tryon home held in the Prince's honor, since then he did not have a wife of his own to act as hostess.

Australian born Dale—nicknamed "Kanga" by Charles—used to accompany her husband and the Prince on fishing trips to Iceland. Charles not only liked her sense of humor but always sought her opinion on his girl friends, including Lady Di.

In typical Aussie style "Kanga" is a down-to-earth girl who speaks plainly and likes her beer. She is full of charm, refreshingly frank, and open. The Tryons have a daughter Zoe, six, and a son Charles, four, to whom Prince Charles is god-father, and twins Victoria and Edward, born in 1980. Lady Tryon never, never talked about Prince Charles's private life. "It is best not to," she said. "So many people ask, but I never say anything."

The other woman he consulted before finally proposing to Diana was Camilla Parker-Bowles, married to the Royal Household Cavalry Officer, Andrew Parker-Bowles. Charles and the Parker-Bowleses used to hunt regularly together in Gloucestershire, and this was one of the reasons why the Prince chose as his new home nearby Highgrove. Newlyweds Charles and Di will have Andrew and Camilla as their neighbors. It was Camilla who had always acted as the country version of Dale Tryon—a close friend able to act as a hostess for Charles and offer useful advice.

VIII

Action Man

Lady Di has always known that she was taking in hand one helluva guy who enjoys risking his royal neck. According to one of her friends: "She knows it is going to be tough, like controlling a wild stallion, I suppose, but she loves him so much that she wants to have not only a happy but long life together."

Among the points that Diana and Charles discussed before the final decision to marry were his daring Action Man–James Bond interests in risking his life. Like any future bride who has admired the virile activities of her husband-to-be before marriage, Diana talked about Charles's constant desire to risk his neck. His penchant for danger had also recently worried the Queen, so Diana now has a strong ally at the palace.

He has risked death at most activities that

could possibly get the royal adrenaline flowing—
and not all of them without nearly breaking that
tough and stubborn neck of his.

As a pilot in both the Royal Navy and Royal
Air Force he has flown every type of aircraft from
commando helicopters to 1,000 mph plus
McDonnell Douglas F4 Phantom jet fighters.

His first parachute jump during his RAF training nearly ended in disaster when he found himself descending upside down toward the sea with
his legs caught in the rigging lines. Despite this,
when he was made colonel-in-chief of the
Parachute Regiment three years ago, he decided
to carry out a full-training program with the other
paras to earn his wings—and his lines got twisted
again on one jump.

He has dived under the Arctic ice, hunted for
Russian submarines as the skipper of a warship,
and has now taken up the dangerous sport of
steeplechasing, the sort of gentleman's caper
made world famous by the death-defying Grand
National at Liverpool every year, which injures
riders and often kills horses.

He spends fifty thousand pounds a year on
keeping a stable of polo ponies—his greatest
extravagance—and on at least two occasions he
has been thrown so badly that he suffered injuries
from being kicked by one of his horses, including
a severe blow to the head.

Steeplechasing with all its risks has become an
obsession with Charles, an obsession that Diana
does not share.

Why does he do these things? According to

Charles: "I always like pushing myself to the limit—just to see how far I can go. I get terrified at times."

According to a psychologist: "He has never been able, until now, to flash a good-looking girl on his arm and say 'Look who I've got, guys—isn't she a knockout?'

"He has never been able to publicly declare that he is in love or having an affair with a girl. He has always been such public property. Risking his neck in dangerous sports has been his way of showing what a virile man he is.

"He could never brag about girl friends, so he has had to show his manliness in other ways."

Prince Charles has always wanted to taste everything life can offer, and with the privileges of his office to help him he has ventured everything and feared naught.

Until the day of his marriage and coronation in Westminster Abbey he had set himself one task above all others. He wished to learn at first hand as much as possible about the people he will one day govern, and the world he will lead. He always wanted to experience as much of life as he could in the years before the responsibilities of marriage and the throne curbed his adventurous spirit.

Queen Elizabeth, the Queen Mother, once said of her grandson: "If there was anything left to discover in the world, Charles would have been an explorer."

The Prince has said: "I like to see if I can challenge myself to do something that is potentially hazardous, just to see if mentally I can accept that challenge and carry it out. I like to try all sorts of things because they appeal to me. I'm one of those people who doesn't like sitting and watching someone else doing something. I don't like going to the races to watch horses thundering up and down. . . . I'd rather be riding the horses myself.''

This dislike of just sitting and watching is demonstrated to the limit when he is on official tours abroad. To him the world appears as a huge adventure playground, with a variety of people to meet and different ways of life to learn.

His special position in society has made it easier for him than most other young men to try his hand at new and often daring experiences. A telephone call from the palace could always fix most things, though much of his activities have been part of his training in the Royal Air Force and Royal Navy. He has been the envy of every schoolboy and a man admired by any adult who ever had Walter Mitty dreams.

During an official visit to Canada, Charles was in the barren northern points of his mother's realm. He visited Resolute Bay in the Northwest Territories in April 1975. He had been a sub-aqua swimmer for several years and could not resist joining a small band of divers who regularly plunge into the chillier parts of the Dominion.

His experience included training to escape from submarines, so he was no stranger to climbing into a frogman's suit. He had enjoyed the water from early childhood when he splashed around the Buckingham Palace pool. Sinking beneath the Arctic ice, however, has always been only for the more daring marine brethren.

He went under the ice with a Canadian scientist, Dr. Joe MacInnes, of Undersea Research Limited, who had his headquarters over a narrow hole in the wasteland, leading down to the chilly depths. The scientist and his assistants were trying to gain a greater understanding of both the surface and underwater aspects of life near the North Pole.

Charles remembered his dive as follows:

"I lowered myself gingerly into the water, which by now was covered with newly formed pieces of ice—rather like crème de menthe frappe—and sank like a great orange walrus into the ice-covered world below. Once at the bottom of the six-foot shaft the similarity with a walrus vanished abruptly to be replaced by a resemblance to a dirigible balloon underwater. I found it extremely hard to preserve my balance and had to struggle to stay upright.

"Despite the rubber hood, the water felt decidedly cold around my mouth and a few other edges, not to mention the fact that with heavy gloves on my hands I could not get my fingers onto my mask in order to clear my ears. I thus 'ballasted' myself out at a depth which was not too painful and took stock of the situation. It was a fascinating eerie world of grayish-greenish light that met my gaze, and above all was the roof of ice which disappeared into the distance.

"The visibility was extraordinarily good. Dr. MacInnes said the water was virtually silt-free due to the lack of wave action—the ambient light visibility was a hundred feet.''

After the Prince got used to swimming around in the strange environment, occasionally using his hands to stop him from bumping his head against the underside of the ice pack, he decided to have some fun. Dr. MacInnes showed him how to do the upside-down walk on the underside of the ice, and he recalled, ''I could not resist giving it a try! The result was comical in the extreme. I only partly succeeded. What was fascinating was to see the exhaust bubbles from the two of us trapped on the underside of the ice spread out like great pools of shimmering mercury.''

The icicles? ''They looked like beautiful transparent wafers. Nestling in the gaps between the wafers were lots of shrimplike creatures.''

His intrepid companion left Prince Charles floating around the craggy undersurface for a few minutes and dived to a shell-shaped station at the bottom of the sea. He returned with a bowler hat on his rubber-capped head and brandishing an umbrella.

The royal frogman reached out a hand, took the umbrella from his scientist friend, and tried his hand at underwater clowning. He opened the umbrella and posed for pictures with Dr. MacInnes.

Now that he was familiar with this jade-colored underworld, he decided to jolly up the adventure a little more. He descended sixty feet to the shelter and entered it through an airlock with his fellow swimmer. Inside, he was shown some of the plants growing in a corner of the structure which was being used as a seabed laboratory. Then, switching to the surface listening post on the telephone link, Charles and the scientist sang The Beatles' song: "We All Live in a Yellow Submarine."

When he returned topside he had another trick up his sleeve. In the tent covering the hole carved into the ice he inflated his orange diving suit to amuse the photographers waiting outside. "The result was astonishing and I looked exactly like M. Michelin," remembered Charles.

The dive into this weird edge of the world lasted around thirty minutes. Forty minutes is considered to be the limit a first-time diver should stay in these scary conditions. It was a worrying time for the accompanying security men waiting nervously on the surface. No detective wanted to go down in history as the man who lost the future King of England—underwater.

To ensure that the Prince's escapade would carry the minimum of risks, the security team and the diving experts worked out in advance a very careful program for the operation, which took place 493 nautical miles north of the Arctic Circle. This included a forty-five-minute check of the battery-powered heated suit and the other equipment to be used. A rescue team stood by ready to go at the first sign of an emergency.

When he made his eight thousand-mile tour around the frozen Northwest Territories, he sampled as much as he could of the land of the Eskimo.

After he walked down the steps of his plane on to a remote airfield, clad in natty fur skin, he was off for a ride on a dog sleigh. He soon got bored with being a passenger. Returning from a six-mile trip over the snow and ice, he asked his Eskimo dog handler to sit in the back and he took over the huskies.

The first time he came across a snowmobile, he "went mad," according to one of the party with him. After rapidly learning how to control the half-tracked vehicle, he accelerated away, ploughing to the front in a race across the ice. "He was laughing and shouting like a cowboy on a bucking bronco as he zipped along at around forty-five miles an hour," said a fellow rider.

Eskimo life fascinated him. He had seen plenty of igloos around but insisted on going inside one of them. It seemed proper to him that he should find out how the most northerly of his future subjects lived.

His hosts also showed him how they built their sparsely furnished dwellings. If an Eskimo is caught in a sudden storm, an igloo is his only protection. Some of them could pile up the chunks of ice into an instant home in as little as fifteen minutes.

He watched Eskimos fishing through the ice for seals. A short time later he came across more than he had bargained for, however, when he saw a demonstration of seal-skinning. A young girl came up to him and offered the local "delicacy"—raw seal meat. "I looked at it and said 'Ugh!' but she kept saying I must eat it,"

Charles remembers. "For the honor of the family I picked up a piece of meat and made the fatal error, of course, of chewing it rather than swallowing it like a sheep's eye.

"The trouble was that it tasted absolutely appalling. I said, 'The press here are going to eat this and all the people with me . . . you'll all eat it.'

"They shrank away and disappeared. A doctor who was with us muttered in their ears that they shouldn't eat it because it was probably a week old. So I said, 'Thank you very much, chummy, what about me? Eh!'"

Dipping a royal foot into the whirlpool of life could be amusing but it also has had its more frightening and discomforting aspects. These the Prince has had to undergo as part of his training in the Royal Navy and Royal Air Force.

Such experiences included a practice submarine underwater escape from one hundred feet down, without any breathing apparatus. Men have died doing the same thing in the Royal Navy's training tank at H.M.S. *Dolphin* at Gosport on the English Channel coast of Hampshire. The Prince had to go through with it to prepare himself for a nuclear submarine patrol.

After "escaping" from depths of thirty, then sixty, feet without breathing equipment, he descended to the base of the practice tank, filled with seven hundred tons of seawater. Wearing a protective suit, goggles, and a clip over his nose, he stepped into an airlock which was a mock-up of the sort found in submarines.

A connecting door was opened and water began to pour in. When it reached his neck, Charles took a deep breath and entered the base of the tank. As the natural buoyancy in his body took him upward, he had to remember to breathe out carefully—"whistling to the top," as the experts call it. If he had not done this, his lungs could have been damaged under the tremendous water pressure or an air bubble might have been forced into his bloodstream, causing a blockage in the heart.

He kept a cool head, remembered all his instructors had taught him, and shot out of the water at the top of the tank like a cork.

Part of his training as a helicopter pilot involved taking part in what the British Royal Marine Commandos call a "Tarzan" course. As a Royal Navy pilot he had to carry the commandos in his aircraft, so the navy chiefs thought it would be a good idea for him and other pilots to get firsthand knowledge of what the British Green Berets got up to. A group of pilots went through the ordeal of a grueling commando endurance test at the Royal Marine training center at Lympstone in Devon.

Charles scaled climbing nets and vertical walls, edged along catwalks, swung across chasms, slid down ropes at death-defying speeds, and crawled from tree to tree on a swaying ropewalk. Then came a mile and a half cross-country slog followed by an even tougher military refinement: He had to crawl through tunnels half-filled with water and one completely filled. At the other end of this one the strong arms of a marine were waiting to pull him through by the scruff of his noble neck.

With typical British understatement the only judgment the Royal Marines would allow themselves after the marathon performance was "The Prince showed he didn't lack physical fitness."

During his earlier RAF training, Charles made a parachute jump from a twin-engined Andover of the RAF Support Command over the English Channel, down to a bay on the Dorset coast. When the plane was in position, at an altitude of twelve hundred feet, a sliding door opened near the tail and the whistle of the slipstream could be heard. Below, the sea looked a long way down.

The dispatcher nodded to Prince Charles that he should get ready and walk to the edge of the heaving doorway. He stood up, steadying himself to get his balance. The static line that would, hopefully, pull out his 'chute as he left the plane was attached to a cable. He checked his reserve 'chute, strapped on the front of his blue flying overalls, and the quick release catch. The dispatcher, Flight Sergeant Ken Kidd, thought he was a little too far from the door, and suggested a few steps forward might be in order.

With less than a minute to go, the Andover began its final run over Studland Bay, a holiday beach near Poole, in the area of the English coast that launched the D Day invasion of Normandy. The Prince gripped the side of the exit. A green light went on and Kidd tapped him on the shoulder and shouted "Go!" Charles jumped without hesitation. With a welcome jerk the Prince felt the canopy open, but then something went wrong and he found himself descending with his legs caught in the rigging.

He kept his cool as he dropped toward splashdown and later recounted the incident objectively: "I determined to myself that I wouldn't think about the jump too much beforehand. Otherwise I would have worried. In the end I stood in the doorway and I didn't need kicking out. I jumped out happily except that after I'd jumped, for some unknown reason—I must have hollow legs or something—my legs went over my head.

"The next thing I knew they were tangled in the rigging lines, so I was looking up at them and coming down in a sort of U shape. I said to myself calmly, 'Your legs are in the rigging so you must remove them.' So I removed them—fortunately—by about eight hundred feet. Then I had a lovely sail down to sea level. Of course I forgot to inflate my life jacket because I'd enjoyed it so much."

When he hit the sea, motor launches, manned by Royal Marines, fished him out of the water within ten seconds and whisked him away for a stiff drink.

In the years since he gained his pilot's license, Charles, as both a civilian pilot and a service flier in the Royal Air Force and the Royal Navy, has flown everything from a helicopter to a jet bomber.

His interest in flying had been encouraged early by his father. Charles was twenty when he first went solo in a single-engine, propeller-driven Chipmunk, emblazoned in red—the color of the Queen's Flight, that elite squadron of the Royal Air Force. He had an immediate aptitude for flying and the men who have accompanied him in the cockpits of many aircraft since then—from the comparatively snaillike Chipmunk to supersonic F4 Phantoms—have all agreed that he is a "natural" airman.

Like every pilot who has had to face up to the final terrifying test of going solo, Prince Charles remembers that moment well. "It's imprinted on my mind indelibly. I suppose I worried about it for a bit . . . the thought of actually having to go solo and whether I was capable of doing it. Whether I'd remember the right things to do.

"But when the day came, the instructor got out of the cockpit, rather surprisingly as I didn't think I was going to do it that day, and said, 'Right—it's your turn!' So I sat there with butterflies in my tummy while he got out and then when I was actually airborne, I was amazed how much more fun it was.

"I flew round and round and admired the scenery. I controlled my butterflies. Then I did a perfect landing as it turned out—I never did a better one after that."

From that day onward, just like his father, flying was in his blood. He could not get enough of it and a spell in the Royal Air Force was inevitable. He wanted to hear the roar of the jet engines and feel the G force pinning him in his seat in a tight aerobatic turn.

Prince Charles joined the RAF at twenty-three. He went to Cranwell, the Air Force college in Lincolnshire—the British Colorado Springs—which has been the training ground for top pilots for nearly fifty years.

He was able to skip ahead somewhat in the Royal Air Force, as he did later in the navy, and only had to go through a streamlined, speeded-up course. As a graduate qualified pilot, he was gazetted as a flight lieutenant (captain) before he set foot in the college. He carried the rings of rank on the sleeves of his uniform as he flew to Cranwell to be inducted into the service.

With perhaps forgivable ostentation he piloted himself there in a twin-engine Bassett light aircraft of the Queen's Flight. Waiting for him, apart from a lineup of top RAF brass, was a five-month program that would bring out in him that excellence needed to qualify for wings in the Royal Air Force. The senior officers who greeted him made it clear that he was going to have to earn his wings: a true case of "Per Ardua ad Astra"—by hard work to reach the stars.

The operation to get the royal pilot to supersonic level was code-named "Exercise Golden Eagle." He became part of the first course made up entirely of university graduates, sharing a flat with three other ex-student cadets, and like them he was subject to service discipline.

Heading toward the stratosphere was Charles's ambition, but before he was allowed to go aloft in one of the two specially maintained Provost jet trainers, he had to go through a grueling test on the ground. He was locked in a decompression chamber, "taken up" to twenty thousand feet in simulated conditions, then ordered to unhook his oxygen mask.

The effect of this is just like the moment before blacking out in the dentist's chair after being given a whiff of anesthetic. A pilot becomes drowsy and quite loses his bearings before feeling himself disappear into a void. Charles had to experience this in the testing chamber so he would recognize the symptoms if his oxygen supply went wrong while he was in the air.

During this oxygen training at an aeromedical training center not far from Cranwell he had to leave his mask off for several minutes and do simple handwriting tests until he was on the verge of blackout. What he wrote during his highly uncomfortable experiment is rumored to be in language appropriate to the discomfort of the time. It is a choice piece of memorabilia which the RAF has tucked safely away for historical purposes.

Although it was not his wish, the air force went to incredible lengths to make sure Charles got through his flying course safely. Radar kept his aircraft under constant surveillance when he was flying, and other aircraft for fifty miles around Cranwell were ordered to keep clear. A maintenance team twice the usual size made sure that the two 480 mph Provost trainers earmarked for him were always in faultless condition. In addi-

Prince Charles and Lady Diana: the official engagement
photo.

Lady Diana with two of her charges at the Young England Kindergarten, September 1980.

Lady Diana before the engagement, 1981.

Prince Charles,
sportsman.

The Royal Family in an informal setting, Balmoral Castle
in Scotland, on the occasion of the thirty-second
anniversary of the wedding of Queen Elizabeth to the Duke
of Edinburgh, November 20, 1979. Left to right: Prince
Philip, Prince Edward, Prince Charles, Queen Elizabeth,
Prince Andrew, and Princess Anne with her son Master
Peter Phillips.

© PRESS ASSOCIATION

Lady Diana's mother,
Mrs. Shand-Kydd, at home.

© PRESS ASSOCIATION LTD.

Lady Diana's father, Earl Spencer, on the grounds of
Althorp, the family home.

Lady Diana and Prince Charles at their first public function together, attending a concert at Goldsmith Hall, London. This strapless gown created quite a stir.

Prince Charles with Lady Diana and the Queen Mother in the paddock at Sandown Park, March 13, 1981.

Highgrove House in the Cotswolds, purchased for Prince Charles and Lady Diana at a cost of $2,000,000.

The yellow bedroom at Highgrove House.

A portrait of the royal couple painted by Judi Mendelsohn, pub owner and artist. She plans to offer it to them as a wedding present.

tion his planes had special red flashing lights fitted to distinguish them from other trainers.

The Junior Service did its best, but the Prince presented them with a major problem that only he could solve. One of the essential qualities for any pilot is a ready understanding of mathematics. Charles, unfortunately, has always been toward the bottom of the class when it came to mental arithmetic and rapid calculation in such boring pastimes as algebraic equations, geometric formulas, and logarithmic tables, a blind spot he shares with the Queen.

As he is the first to admit: "Maths taken in its pure context is misery, I think. I find it boring. I'm one of those people who prefers ideas rather than numbers. I could never understand maths. I always thought it was the way I'd been taught originally that made me so hopeless, but on the other hand, perhaps I just don't have a mathematical mind."

Prince royal or not, a pilot without some skill in mathematics was of no use to the Royal Air Force. He just had to get up to scratch. He put his head down and, fighting his way through a battlefield of unfriendly figures, managed to reach a math standard that satisfied his instructors. Even today, though, he says with remarkable honesty, "From the flying point of view my arithmetic is not as fast as some other people's."

Once in the cockpit of a jet trainer, with the controls in his hands, the natural talent he has above zero feet flashed through. He quickly got the hang of flying jets and was soon learning the aerobatics needed by a jet-age fighter pilot. He made his first solo flight after only eight hours' instruction instead of the usual ten.

The Prince wanted to get a taste of all the aircraft being flown by the RAF during the short time he would be able to spend in the service. With his excellent record as a pilot to back him up, he could make a good claim to get his hands on the more exotic hardware.

Just a few weeks after he had gone solo, Charles copiloted an F4 Phantom of Forty-three—"The Fighting Cocks" squadron from Leuchars in Scotland. He took part in a scramble and an interception over the North Sea with another Phantom acting as "the enemy," then his aircraft nudged in carefully behind a Victor flyer tanker to take on twelve hundred gallons of fuel—one of the hairiest of airborne maneuvers. Few pilots like doing this because of the risk of an explosive collision.

He flew as high as forty thousand feet and as low as one thousand feet when he made a pass over the Royal Family's castle at Balmoral in a final flourish. When he landed, he was made a member of the exclusive Ten Ton Club—that enviable group who have piloted a plane at more than 1,000 mph.

The next day he sat in a more spacious cockpit, alongside the captain of a Nimrod NATO maritime reconnaissance aircraft, for a day-long patrol over the Atlantic. For four hours he piloted this four-engine jet, whose main function is the detection, and in wartime the destruction, of submarines. With sophisticated radar and under-water search equipment just one Nimrod can monitor the surface and undersea movements of the entire Mediterranean in a few high-flying min-utes.

The Prince then rounded off his tropospheric education a week later in a nuclear bomber. He copiloted a Vulcan, the delta-wing aircraft that is the mainstay of the British strategic strike force. With four powerful engines it travels at just under the speed of sound with a frightening destructive capability of either missiles, hydrogen bombs, or twenty-one thousand pounds worth of what are chillingly called "conventional" bombs.

The citizens of Doncaster, an industrial town in the north of England, were not aware of it at the time, but they had the privilege of being the target when their future King made a high-level dummy attack on them.

It was to be another five years, after his naval service, before he got the chance to fly a jet again. He went back to Cranwell in February 1977—now a wing commander (lieutenant colonel)—to brush up his basic flying and aerobatics. "I've forgotten so much," he said. "Especially those convolutions of the stomach when you go into a roll or a loop. Dangerous? No, it's more dan-gerous crossing the road."

For his helicopter training, Charles joined the aptly named Red Dragon—of Wales—flight of Number 707 naval squadron at Yeovilton in Somerset, right in the heart of Britain's West Country. He was trained to handle one of the most difficult aircraft to fly, the big Sikorsky S-58 Wessex helicopters.

For three and a half months he worked hard at getting the hang of controlling and navigating a Wessex in all weathers and over any type of terrrain. Mountain flying was the most difficult and the most hazardous. He did this among the peaks of his own principality of Wales, actually landing on top of its highest peak three-thousand-foot Mount Snowdon.

He trained in air-sea rescue work, learning to maneuver just above wave tops, blinded by the spray his own rotors were throwing up, in order to winch volunteers to safety from the water. Charles was also taught how to fire weapons such as rockets and guided missiles, and how to take commandos into battle.

After 105 flying hours spread over forty-five days he went solo and qualified as an operational helicopter combat pilot—ready for anything, anywhere in the world.

Red Dragon flight became a front-line squadron on board the commando carrier H.M.S. *Hermes*. Charles and the rest of the newly trained pilots were taken to the other side of the Atlantic. They flew in the subtropical climate of the Caribbean and below zero temperature in northern Canada.

Helicopter flying became the greatest thrill of his life. He said at the time, "It's very challenging. There's that superb mixture of fear and enjoyment which comes over me. . . . It is marvelous when things are going right and you can pick up a reference on the ground and not bother with the map. Then that panic when you don't really know where you are and you've got to sort it out yourself. It's so exciting.

"I've given myself a fright or two. The other day we were going along quite well when flames suddenly started to shoot out of the engine on my side, making extraordinary 'whoof-whoof' noises. All the instruments were twitching away.

"Fortunately, I was with the senior pilot of the squadron, so we shut down the engine and landed in a ploughed field beside a motorway—much to everybody's amazement!"

On another occasion, though, he admitted, "It's bloody terrifying sometimes."

Because of his amazing attraction to dangerous sports Prince Charles has suffered many an injury and ailment. But he always goes back for more.

From an early age Charles sported bumps and bruises resulting from his father's wish that the young prince give up his music and dancing lessons and get used to the rough and tumble of tough physical activity. When he was seventeen he broke his nose while playing an over-enthusiastic game of rugby at his tough public school. He was later put out of action again with a bout of pneumonia after an adventure camping holiday with his schoolfriends. June 1972 found him sporting an embarrassing look because of a sticking plaster covering a graze on his chin: he had got in the way of a fast-moving polo ball during a practice game.

He has certainly become the macho type man that his father always wanted to see.

One of the nicknames given to Charles recently has been "Action Man," and he hates the title. Yet there seems to have been no stopping his daredevilry. Four years of skiing in Switzerland have been getting more exciting as he graduated to the most dangerous runs around Klosters. He had the occasional fall, but his answer has always been to keep going—"We British have to ski on, don't we?"—then rub liniment on his bruises later that night in the chalet.

Last year Prince Charles suffered several mishaps while playing polo. In April he was rushed to hospital in Florida after he nearly fainted from heat exhaustion and fatigue while playing a polo match at Palm Beach. Some of the people watching thought that going onto the polo field after a jet-lagged flight across the Atlantic may even have caused a mild heart attack, but this was never confirmed.

Back in England he has taken several tumbles, including being thrown by his pony and kicked in the face. And that's not counting the four falls he's had in a dangerous cocktail of fox-hunting and steeplechasing called "eventing."

His polo handicap was recently raised from three to four, putting him within reach of international class. Only seven other British players rank higher in the sport. (In polo, unlike golf, the higher the handicap the better.)

Diana is not as keen on horses as Charles and other members of his family, but it looks as though she is going to have to show more interest—just like any other new wife whose husband is sports crazy.

Charles once said: "I love the game, I love the ponies and I love the exercise. It's my favorite game." He has played it all over the world, including India, where the game was originated and brought to Europe by the officers of the British raj in the nineteenth century.

Charles has been playing polo since he was sixteen and keeps a string of ponies at Windsor. He learned to ride ten years earlier on a small Shetland pony he used to gently trot across Windsor Great Park, where he now gallops. He mounted up for his first chukka while he was at Gordonstoun School. His father captained a team of novices, including Charles, who had the excitement of scoring a goal on his very first outing.

Although he is by nature a modest person, he has succumbed to temptation now and again and put on a bit of a show on the polo field if a girl friend was watching.

One of the regular players with Charles says, "He is absolutely fearless. He is very aggressive and thunders along at a frightening pace. Over the past ten years he has become a player of top international class."

This frightening pace may account for his recent run of tumbles. And he hasn't escaped them all lightly. The most serious was when he was thrown and trampled in a practice game and ended up with that hoof-shaped bruise near his heart and the cut that required nine stitches near his left ear. He also has a small scar near his left eye as a result of another fall at polo.

He recently took up what—until pure steeplechasing—must have been one of his most dangerous pursuits; cross-country eventing, in which teams of four ride two and a half miles across rough country at breakneck speed over twenty-five jumps.

But until his marriage plans were announced at least, he had even more spectacular plans for himself. Having ridden in a flat race at Plumpton and over the fences in National Hunt racing at Sandown, he fancies his chances in the Grand National. He has told organizers in Liverpool that he would like a shot at the world's toughest race, but the Queen is understood to be against the idea, saying, ''That's enough, Charles!''

Whether or not he'll take heed of her or his new wife is yet to be seen, but certainly there will come the day when he must accept that enough is absolutely and utterly enough, and opt at last for more sedate pastimes. Until then Diana can only hold her breath every time he leaps out of a plane, gallops across the polo grounds, dives under the polar icecap, or goes mountain climbing.

As his experiences under the ice in Canada showed, he is a highly skilled diver. Both at home and abroad he has explored old wrecks among the weeds and rocks on the bottom of numerous seas.

Charles writes about these experiences in emotive prose. He once recalled his diving as ''describing the supreme fascination of life below the waves.''

Recounting some of his adventures in the journal of the British Sub-Aqua Club, *Diver,* he mentioned exploring a wreck off the British Virgin Islands—"experiencing the extraordinary sensation of swimming inside the hull of an old schooner as if it was some vast green cathedral filled with shoals of fish."

He once came up with pieces of eight and musket balls from a seventeenth-century wreck off the Colombian coast and plunged more than fifty feet to the muddy seabed at Spithead near Southampton to look at a four hundred-year-old naval relic, the *Mary Rose.* One of his companions described him as "an exceptional diver."

His taste for danger, he says, "tends to make you appreciate life that much more and to really want to live it to the fullest."

When Charles, or any member of the Royal Family, goes flying, either by helicopter or in fixed-wing aircraft, they travel in the most carefully monitored airspace in the world, just like *Air Force One.* They are given a flight path exclusive to themselves, and no other aircraft is allowed to enter or cross it. That section of the sky becomes known as the Purple Airway, out of bounds to even a plane or helicopter on a mercy mission.

It seems likely that his wild horsemanship will continue and Diana will have to sit on the sidelines and worry alongside her mother-in-law. But jumping out of aircraft and diving under polar icecaps are probably over for good. It is going to be hard for Charles to accept, but with children more than likely on the way within a few years he is going to have to become a responsible family man.

He will never be the boring middle-aged pipe-and-slippers sort—but the parachute has more than likely been hung up forever.

With the lovely Diana to distract him it's not going to be too much of a sacrifice.

IX

Navy Days

Treat 'em mean and keep 'em keen'' about sums up the hardy old seadog philosophy of Britannia Royal Naval College, Dartmouth—the British Annapolis. It is a view of life shared by the officers on the staff, who deal out a formidable amount of that meanness.

Britannia, or the Stone Frigate as she has been called by generations of naval officers who have suffered on her parade ground, lies among the flower beds and green acres alongside the River Dart in an otherwise delightful part of Devon in Britain's West Country.

Its primary task is to train and lick into shape the successors to Admiral Nelson. It has been the finishing school for future British kings for almost a century. The sons of the monarchy go there to have teen-age spots knocked off them and be submitted to harsh discipline.

Prince Charles's ancestors all had to go through it. His father, Prince Philip; his grandfather, George VI; his great-grandfather, George V; and his great-great-grandfather, Edward VII. All had the final touches of royal luster painfully varnished on them there. Young Charles had to brace up to it in his turn.

King George V insisted in his day that a spell before the mast—Conrad style—was essential for young princelings to prepare themselves for royal duties. Prince Charles still supports this view, and it is not without significance that Prince Andrew, his younger brother, has had to go through the same training.

On one occasion, toward the end of his career at sea, he said: "I feel that if one is going to get involved in the whole spectrum of life in this country, then one should get to know about the Services. One should get to know about the navy particularly, because ultimately our security and everything depends upon the navy. It always has done throughout history and always will. Therefore it is very important to know about it. Having learnt at school that discipline exists, and I'm highly disciplined myself, it helped me in the navy."

Charles went to Dartmouth in the late summer of 1971 to prepare himself for the five years he was to spend as a Royal Navy officer in what will one day be his King's Navy, to learn at every level from bridge to lower deck the operations and the cherished legends of Britain's Senior Service.

He had already served at the Royal Air Force College, Cranwell, won his wings, and graduated from Cambridge University with a Bachelor of Arts degree. Because of these qualifications he did not have to join the navy as an ordinary cadet. Acting as a sub-lieutenant, the Prince of Wales was among a dozen university graduate officers who "went aboard" Britannia to take a cram six-week course before going into various branches of the Royal Navy.

He had a twelve-hour nonstop day from early morning until dusk. Before seven each morning his steward, Joseph Atkinson, woke him up with just enough time to reach breakfast in the sub-lieutenants' mess. Mr. Atkinson kept the Prince's cabin tidy, but the young officer had to polish his own shoes and keep his own clothes and uniforms smart.

Charles and the other officers had barely time to swallow their breakfasts before being put through the paces on a half hour of marching gymnastics. The man in charge of the drill, Lieutenant Peter Richardson, said at the time: "We have no special attitudes towards graduates. They get kicked to death like any other man. But I think most people enjoy it. It can be fun."

With just a short time available, the instructors tried to make the Prince and his classmates worthy of command. On the parade ground there were three hour-long sessions each week in addition to the daily parades, including marching, standing to attention, saluting, and, even in the age of nuclear submarines, sword drill. None of Her Majesty's officers are expected to survive without eighteenth-century sword drill!

In the gymnasium there were at least two hour-long sessions every week, planned, according to one of the sports officers, "so that one reaches the limit of one's endurance in a very short space of time." For his first swimming test Charles had to swim four hundred meters in a boiler suit, float for three minutes, then dive to the bottom of the college pool and pick up a brick eight feet down. He also learned lifesaving and how to give mouth-to-mouth resuscitation on a blond Swedish dummy known to the cadets as "Resusci-Anne."

But most of the busy days were spent in classrooms, learning the textbook techniques of life at sea, and studying navigation, weaponry, marine and electrical engineering, administration, and management. This sort of training certainly puts this prince a cut above the rest.

It was rough going, but in the end Prince Charles got through his first major test as a naval officer. Under a peevishly dull sky on the last Friday of October 1971 he and his fellow graduate officers led the passing-out parade of five hundred officer cadets while the band played, appropriately, "God Bless the Prince of Wales."

Watching with pride was Charles's late great-uncle, Admiral of the Fleet, Earl Mountbatten of Burma. This dashing naval giant, and World War II leader, had always been among those members of the Royal Family who wanted the Prince to "go away to sea."

The Royal Navy was a career that Charles enjoyed, although a profession he was allowed to follow for only a brief time because of the other demands of apprentice kingship. Thanks to the family tradition the Royal Navy meant a great deal. Its history of smoke, cannon, and valor interested him.

The rewards of serving in it excited him and gave the navy a chance to get to know him. He had the opportunity to meet his future subjects at close hand. There were few secrets in some of the tiny ships he served in. He got used to living at close quarters with everyone from the jolly old chaps out of the well-bred households that have always supplied Britain's officer class, to the occasionally fruity-tongued "Jack" whose mum and dad might live in tenements.

"You're all together out there at sea, in that small community, cut off," he said. "It's a very intense communal life."

He might have been a prince ashore, but during his naval duties he appeared on ships' crew lists as either sub-lieutenant, or later Lieutenant Charles Windsor (using the family surname). As such he received the same treatment and work-load as any other officer, including those exhausting nightly "dog watches." As a junior officer he became responsible for the welfare, as well as discipline, of as many as thirty men under him.

This included helping them sort out their per-

sonal problems, whether they be debts, trouble
with girl friends, worries about their marriages, or
even the sad task of telling a man that a relative
had died. "Where else could a future king learn
how difficult it is to keep a wife and family
together during long separations and on a limited
budget?" pointed out one of his captains.

He soon got the hang of getting on with the
seamen he commanded. After five weeks at sea in
his first ship, the guided missile destroyer H.M.S.
Norfolk, he came ashore at Portsmouth Dockyard
(Britain's Brooklyn Navy Yard) for a few days'
leave. A rating who, like the rest of the four-
hundred-odd men on board, had been watching
closely the way the newcomer found his sea legs
said: "The lads like him. He listens to you . . .
you don't think of him as royalty," and added,
"He's a good shipmate!"

The "good shipmate" also showed he could
mix in socially with the best of them when he
went to the *Norfolk*'s annual dance, an occasion
very special to the crew, a big night out ashore
with all their wives and girl friends. Prince
Charles was a familiar face among the crush at
the local *palais de danse.* Wearing his sub-lieutenant's uniform, he danced with the wives of
fellow officers and ratings and dipped his hand
into his pocket to pay for his share of drinks.

The three years following that marching-out
parade at Dartmouth were mainly spent at sea, in
a great variety of ships, learning the profession of
being a naval officer in all parts of the world.
He gained his watch-keeping certificate—the

Royal Navy's "driver's license"—during the nine months he was in the *Norfolk*. This qualified him to be in complete charge of a ship, responsible for every decision he ordered as officer-of-the-watch on the bridge.

During these three years, and all his time at sea, he was spared none of the duties the other officers had to carry out. Yet at the same time, he still had his royal functions. He had to study state papers, stored in specially secured safes in his various cabins, keep up with the administration of his estates, and handle the usual heavy load of royal correspondence.

While other officers could relax in the ward-room, he caught up with briefings on state affairs, read reports and recommendations from his staff at Buckingham Palace or the London offices of his estates, the Duchy of Cornwall, and decided on the hundreds of requests received every year from all nature of organizations and societies for his royal patronage and support.

Whenever his ship reached port, there would usually be a bag of official papers waiting for him at the end of the gangplank. There would also be one of his armed private detectives, who had flown ahead of him. The Royal Navy was expected to look after the future King at sea, but, in this unpredictable age of the assassin, there was always tight security ashore. Away from the freedom of life at sea he became once more a royal personage, one of the privileged few, a man of power and, therefore, a potential target, just as much as a U.S. president.

Charles, like other members of his family, often receives threats to his life. Most of them are ignored, while a few have to be taken seriously. In these cases Scotland Yard's famous Special Branch makes a few discreet inquiries about whichever crank has got a grudge against the Prince. When the Royals visit anyplace in the world, whether it be Washington or a suburb of London, security checks are made on people living locally who have been known to send off warnings of foul deeds ahead. They are then put under unobtrusive surveillance.

On trips abroad the local police usually carry out the same rigid procedures at the request of the Yard. But the public as a whole, and the many people who come close to the Queen and her family, cannot all be screened by the security people. Opportunities for a sudden attack on heads of state and their families have become greater in recent years because of both the presidential and queenly habit of going on "walkabouts" among crowds. Charles is particularly fond of mixing in with the people, as he once showed while chatting to women and children in a stroll around the ancient streets of Windsor. It was a security man's nightmare—anyone in the crowd could have assaulted him.

The threat of an assassination attempt is always there—a danger that Charles has experienced at least once in a violent and dramatic way, when a naval officer attacked him one night while he was asleep.

It happened in April 1974, shortly after

Princess Anne and her husband Captain Mark Phillips were held at gunpoint in the Mall, a bare few yards from the haven of Buckingham Palace, during a fruitless single-handed kidnap attempt. At the time, Charles was a lieutenant on the frigate H.M.S. *Jupiter,* which had just returned to Plymouth after a world cruise. He was away from the ship taking a course on underwater warfare at Portland, Dorset, and had been allocated quarters ashore in RN barracks.

Around two o'clock in the morning the Prince was awakened by a sound in the sitting room adjoining his bedroom. As he opened the connecting door, he saw a figure rushing toward him.

His attacker and the Prince began to struggle in the darkness. The other man picked up a chair and was about to smash it over Charles's head when he was grabbed from behind. Charles's rescuer was Inspector Paul Officer, one of the royal bodyguards who had been sleeping in a nearby bedroom.

Having heard shouts and furniture being knocked over, the burly six-foot-two-inch detective burst in on the grappling pair, and he and Charles overpowered the man.

Within minutes they were joined by RN police and, screaming and yelling, the intruder was dragged away. He turned out to be another lieutenant who had suddenly become mentally unbalanced. A doctor was called to examine Charles, and although he was shaken, he suffered nothing more serious than slight bruising.

A secret inquiry into the incident revealed that

the fellow officer had been suffering from a hitherto-unnoticed mental illness. He was committed to a service psychiatric hospital.

Because this happened on a quiet service dockyard, well away from the public, it was easy for the authorities to hush up the incident. Newspaper headlines about attempts to kill royalty are considered by the men responsible for guarding them as likely to only encourage further attempts. So there was a blackout, which still exists today, on any official information.

One of the sad lessons for Charles and the men responsible for protecting him was that they could never be too careful in the future. On board ship, surrounded by well-disciplined crew, had always been throught one of the safest possible situations. Now even this had a high-risk factor. Security afloat and ashore was tightened up, and Charles and his detectives rehearsed how to react to various forms of attack. They studied and practiced how and where Charles would dodge, dive, and weave faced with gunmen, bombs, or straightforward physical violence.

Despite this always-present danger ashore and the extra royal work afloat, he managed to collect a seabag full of happy memories and adventures on *Jupiter,* his fourth ship. He went halfway around the world in this 2,450-ton frigate, flying first to join her in the Far East, then sailing across the Pacific to the West Coast of America, and through the Panama Canal for the return Atlantic journey to Britain.

For much of the four months on board he was

the radio officer, but he also took his turn on the bridge, taking the responsibility of watch-keeping. He was not long out from Singapore one stormy day in the South Java Sea when he helped to rescue the twelve-man crew of a tug in distress.

While he was manning the bridge the radio room picked up S.O.S. signals from the stricken Singapore tug *Mediator,* which had gone aground in the storm. Prince Charles ordered a change of course to the scene and alerted the skipper, Commander John Gunning, who joined him on the bridge. The captain backed the young officer's decision and sent off the ship's tiny Wasp helicopter on a search sortie in the driving rain. The pilot, Lieutenant Lawrence Hopkins, spotted the tug and its two barges being battered in the foul weather.

It required seven airborne attempts to put a boarding party with towing lines on the tug and barges. Then after four hours of dangerous, tough work in fiery conditions, *Jupiter* and her men freed the vessel and pulled them to a safe anchor-age. Such was the anonymity of Charles as just another officer doing his job that it is doubtful even today that those twelve men realize what royal hand came to their rescue.

By this time he had been promoted—he was Lieutenant Charles Windsor. The crew had, however, given the Prince of Wales another name—"Taffy Windsor," noting the usual first name of a Welshman, "Taffy."

When the *Jupiter* reached the other side of the Pacific and was taking part in exercises with the

United States Navy in California's San Diego Bay, the Welsh lieutenant saved the ship from what could have been a disastrous collision with another warship.

He was navigating officer, keeping a close watch on the radar in thick fog, when he spotted the blip of the other ship on the screen, heading straight toward *Jupiter*. The other vessel was the U.S.S. *Grindley,* more than twice the size and weight of the British vessel. Charles flashed off urgent signals and, with hasty maneuvering, the two missed each other by forty feet.

Charles spent five years in the Royal Navy, until he reached the level of being the captain of his own ship. In the New Year of 1976 he was eventually given his own command, after studying at the navy's senior "university," the Royal Naval College, Greenwich.

With Britain's small navy of today there are few ships of any size around to put in the hands of a prince. In the end Charles became the skipper of one of the smallest ships in the fleet, H.M.S. *Bronington*.

The 360-ton *Bronington*—named after a Welsh village—is a wooden-hulled minehunter. When Charles joined her, she had such a bad reputation for unsteadiness because of her flat bottom that she was said to "roll on wet grass." Her nickname in the service was "Old Quarter-past-eleven"—her pennant number was 1115.

During his ten months on board he often had great difficulty controlling the ship in even the slightest hint of bad weather. She became the only ship in his entire naval career to make him seasick, a malady he could claim to have shared with Nelson. She was so tough to handle that when he docked her at Rosyth after his first ten weeks at sea as skipper, he said, "They took ten years off my life. . . . I feel about eighty."

The *Bronington* was a workhorse, given the tasks that the larger vessels could not be bothered with. Charles took her minehunting, and blew up the odd mine. For two days he shadowed a Russian submarine caught prowling around Britain's coast and North Sea oil rigs.

He zigzagged among the supertankers and large cargo vessels passing through the world's busiest—and riskiest—seaway, the Straits of Dover. He was there to check on "rogue" skippers, who were not keeping to the navigation rules.

He took part in NATO exercises, bringing his thirty-six-man crew to battle stations against mock attacks by "Russian ships."

Charles, with his sense of humor and fine skill at getting on with people, was a popular skipper. When he gave up his command at the end of 1976, he had a rousing send-off from his shipmates. They hung a black polished lavatory seat around his neck with "H.M.S. *Bronington*" inscribed on it in gold letters, to remind him of the weight of the throne!

It is still one of his most treasured possessions, and one that Lady Diana, Princess of Wales, is going to have to get used to as a reminder of her husband's more boisterous past—afloat.

X

His Difficult Choice

Charles always knew that the girl he would choose as his queen would have to be a rare creature. Well bred enough to understand her place and the place of others in England's complex class structure, resilient enough to project a brave face to the world while under stress. His future bride had to be charming, elegant, worldly, caring, motherly, beautifully groomed, and above all learn all the attributes of stateswomanship, tact, and diplomacy needed to be the woman behind the King.

Charles also realized full well that his position was vastly different from that of his sister. Anne could marry a commoner because she was not immediate heir to the throne. He was in a unique position. He could consider a commoner, but regal traditions made such a choice very difficult for him.

On one of the many occasions when he was asked about the girl he would marry, the Prince answered, "This is awfully difficult because you have to remember that when you marry in my position you are going to marry someone who perhaps one day is going to be Queen.

"I've got to choose somebody very carefully, I think, who could fill this particular role and it has got to be somebody pretty special. I often feel I would like to marry somebody English or perhaps Welsh. Well, British anyway."

The age of the arranged marriage had passed, however. Such has been the affection among the British people for their Royal Family that his future subjects would only want Charles to marry a woman he truly loved, who would give him the strength of a happy home life and support him with her affection while he carries out the onerous duties of kingship.

Diana, Charles has obviously discovered, fits the bill, but despite all those willing girl friends he was always under severe restrictions.

It is one of the ironies of Charles's life that he has become a latter-day defender of the king that history has declared insane, George III.

George, long since known as the "Mad King," reigned from 1770 to 1820. He was held responsible for, among many monarchical errors, the loss of the American colonies and a prolonged war with France. Writers, diarists, and politicians of the day generally pronounced him to be a lunatic.

During one of his typical fits of pique he forced through Parliament a piece of legislation, which, more than two hundred years later, is one of the major obstacles in allowing Prince Charles to marry whomever he wished.

George was annoyed because two of his sons married commoners, so in 1772 he promulgated the Royal Marriage Act. Under this law "no descendant of George II shall be capable of contracting matrimony without the previous consent of the king, and signified under the Great Seal, declared in Council and entered in the Privy Council books." (The Privy Council is the group of distinguished men who traditionally advise British monarchs.)

In less formal language it meant that Charles, as heir in direct line to Mad George's father, was in the hands of his mother and Parliament when it came to picking a bride. He could not simply take the girl around for tea one Sunday afternoon to meet the family. He had to satisfy the requirements of the Queen, the House of Lords, and the House of Commons.

Until the age of twenty-five he could only marry with the consent of the Queen. If she had refused permission, he could still ask for the approval of both Houses of Parliament. Had the Queen turned down his choice, it seemed highly unlikely that even in this democratic age the Lords and the Commons would approve of the match if the girl was so eminently unsuitable to be formally rejected by Her Majesty.

George's parchment of marital mischief was

just one of several archaic laws that held in check Charles's rights as a suitor. The only regal legislation that did not seem to apply to him was the Statute of Treasons passed in 1351, which fussed over the chastity of ladies royal and promised the chopping block or gallows for any overamorous seducer of princesses.

The laws restricting his freedom govern not only the religion, but even the color of his bride-to-be. Under an Act of 1689 she had to be a white Anglo-Saxon Protestant, so there would have been just as big a fuss if he cast his eyes toward a Negress, Arab, or Asian as if he had fallen for a Roman Catholic. This famous—or infamous—Bill of Rights also demanded that Charles declare himself an "enemy of the Catholic religion." Needless to say, it was passed at a time of great religious intolerance in England.

With its intentions, however, according to some experts, it ruled out a Roman Catholic changing her religion, or merely agreeing to have the children brought up according to the teachings of the Church of England. Unless this law is repealed in an era when both churches are getting closer together, Charles, after his coronation, must speak out against the Roman Catholic doctrines of Transubstantiation, the Roman saints, and the sacrifice of the mass. To make the path of love even harder, this act made it quite clear that he would lose his crown if he married a "papist."

This risk to his throne was made still clearer in the Act of Succession of 1701, the law from which Charles would be given the legal authority to rule.

This act invokes the outdated Bill of Rights as the source for its insistence that he should forfeit his crown by marrying a Roman Catholic. To enable Charles to have a Roman Catholic queen, Parliament would have needed to pass new laws either repealing the earlier acts altogether or at least amending those passages which would seem offensive to a large percentage of the non-Protestant population of Britain and the Commonwealth.

A future queen who was Roman Catholic, therefore, looked out of the question, unless Charles contemplated abdication. He takes the role of continuing the royal lineage of the House of Windsor so seriously, and regards his own part in the destiny of his family so highly, however, that abandoning the throne for love was never part of his character.

If he had so drastically followed the example of his great-uncle, the Duke of Windsor, and put love before the throne, it would probably have endangered the British monarchy altogether. Two abdications in forty years could have jeopardized the monarchical system in Britain forever.

Because of his very responsible attitude toward his duties as heir, all the speculation during 1977 about a betrothal to twenty-three-year-old Roman Catholic Princess Marie-Astrid of Luxembourg eventually angered him, although he always took an amused view of speculation on his marriage prospects. Every few months a new name kept popping up in the world's gossip columns; some of them girls he has been genuinely fond of, but many he hardly knew.

He greeted most of this speculation with wry amusement and when the gossip about his sexual prowess got a little too out of hand, he took it in his stride. He once shrugged his shoulders and said, in the manner of a much slandered film star, ''The time to get anxious, in a way, is when nobody's interested at all.''

The ''Astrid Affair,'' as it became known at Buckingham Palace, was too much, however, and it raised his hackles in a most untypical way. One reason was that he had never even contemplated marrying her. He had met Marie-Astrid on only three occasions and he could not remember these clearly. Despite this, gossip columnists at home and abroad persisted in linking pretty, fair-haired ''Asty,'' as she became known, with Charles.

Hadn't the Queen and Prince Philip visited her father and mother the Grand Duke and Grand Duchess in Luxembourg? Then the Grand Duke popped over to Sandringham for a spot of shooting with Prince Philip. The Grand Duke had, after all, been educated at one of Britain's leading Roman Catholic public schools, Ampleforth, in Yorkshire. During the Second World War he became a private in the Irish Guards, carrying out sentry duties at Buckingham Palace. Surely he qualified as the perfect father of a future Queen of the United Kingdom?

Charles himself had said: ''The one advantage of marrying a princess, for instance, or somebody from a Royal Family, is that they know what happens." Surely, said the gossip writers, that was significant.

Then Marie-Astrid went to Cambridge to take an English language course. More gossip. She was also a direct descendant of Charles I of England.

Talks between Roman Catholic and Church of England representatives over the sticky matter of religious difficulties were reported to have taken place. Experts on the delicate subtleties of royal accession were roped in to give their opinion that Astrid need not renounce her Catholicism. Girl-children of the marriage could remain attached to Rome while boys could satisfy the Church of England by becoming Protestant.

Should girls-only be the result of the proposed "union," then the line of succession could pass to Charles's younger brother Prince Andrew— hopefully with a spouse who was a fine upstanding Protestant.

Despite denials from Buckingham Palace about any romance, the rumors continued.

When the gossip and rumor-mongering reached its peak four years ago, Charles ordered the Queen's press secretary at the time, Ronald Allison, to put out an official denial of any romance with Marie-Astrid.

Charles told an acquaintance later, "What could I do throughout the entire period of these rumors? I'm sure Marie-Astrid is a marvelous young woman, but I hardly know her. At the same time, it would have been highly discourteous of me to start putting out denials while the talk was merely gossip.

"This could have been interpreted by some as me saying publicly that a European princess was not good enough for me. I didn't want to offend her and I thought the whole business was highly amusing until things became too much."

During the week that the denial was issued, he still kept tongues wagging by being seen with two perfectly eligible young ladies: Lady Camilla Fane, daughter of the Earl of Westmorland . . . and Lady Sarah Spencer.

XI

The Prince Decides

Diana drove home from her kindergarten and prepared for the evening of February 6, 1981, with special care. She chose a long evening gown for what was to be the most important night of her life. This time there was no long motorway drive. The rendezvous was very close, hardly enough distance to warm up the engine of her British Leyland car. No one noticed her slip away from the mansion block in the Old Brompton Road, clutching a small evening bag, a warm coat around her shoulders.

The policeman in the green Buckingham Palace security post at the big wrought-iron gate nearest to Royal Green Park waved her straight through. He had been warned to expect the red Metro at 8:00 P.M. and Lady Diana was right on time.

She drove through an archway into a small

quadrangle, where her distinctive car would be hidden from the view of the railings at the front. A footman opened the door to the billiard-room entrance but Lady Diana didn't need to be shown the way to the small apartment at one corner of the huge palace: she had been to Prince Charles's private rooms as a guest before that night.

The Prince of Wales, formally dressed in a dark suit, was waiting for her in the small, plainly furnished sitting room of the three-room bachelor flat, overlooking The Mall, the flat he had occupied since the age of twenty-one. A small round table was set for supper with a white linen cloth, silver cutlery, a bowl of flowers, and a single candlestick.

Charles and Diana sat side-by-side on a small satin-covered sofa, chatting, making small talk about his skiing trip, anything that came to mind. They had missed each other and there was a lot of news to catch up on.

Diana later told friends that the Prince seemed very nervous; perhaps at the last minute he was having second thoughts. After all a marriage by the heir to the throne was a marriage for life; there could be no turning back, no divorce. He had once said those oft-quoted words that "about thirty" was the best time to wed and now he was about to take that momentous step, losing his freedom after a full and exciting life as a virtual playboy. He was bound to have butterflies in his stomach.

Diana too felt terribly nervous. As she told her father afterward she was so frightened and excited at the same time that the evening passed in an odd dreamy way as if she weren't actually there at all; it was as if she were standing back watching another girl sitting at that beautifully laid supper table.

A servant had lit the single candle and served a simple meal ending with cheese and fruit, but later Diana couldn't recall what they ate at all.

Over the flattering candlelight the Prince popped the question. The actual words will remain their secret but after the "will you," Charles gave Diana time to think. He didn't expect an answer immediately; he expected her to at least say that she wanted to go away and give it some thought, and was a little taken aback when the blond teen-ager, her blue eyes sparkling in the flickering candlelight, said yes. She had already made up her mind long before the night of February 6 that she was deeply in love with the Prince and wanted to be his bride.

They kissed and talked and talked about their future, about their plans and their hopes. There was an awful lot of planning to do and the single candle on the uncleared supper table had almost burned out by the time Diana drove home.

Prince Charles went about the business of planning his forthcoming marriage in a very old-fashioned, very proper manner. The proposal had been romantic and perfect and he was going to make sure that he did everything else in a gentlemanly manner too.

First he went to see his own parents to tell them the good news. The Queen and Prince Philip were both delighted. The Queen had already told other members of the Royal Family that Lady Diana, who of course she had known as a child, was a "perfectly delightful young lady," and after Diana had joined them at Sandringham, the Queen had made it quite clear that she thought the teen-ager would make a perfect bride for her eldest son.

Then in the proper English manner, Prince Charles had to ask Diana's father for his formal consent. Etiquette specifies that the Prince should have gone to see the fifty-seven-year-old Earl of Spencer at his home. A romantic novelist would have put the two men in armchairs over a glass of port with the Earl asking, "Now, young man, what are your intentions?"

In fact it didn't work out like that at all. Charles made a slightly more modern approach to ask for the lady's hand in marriage. He used the telephone.

The Earl answered the phone at his London flat just across from the American Embassy in Grosvenor Square. Prince Charles called the Earl "Sir" with a nice old-fashioned touch, and the two men laughed over the slightly ludicrous situation as the Prince formally asked the question that the Earl had expected since Christmas. "Over Christmas I realized Diana was in love," said the Earl as the Prince told him, "I would like to marry your daughter, Diana, who much to my astonishment has already said yes."

Later the Earl, who has a fine sense of fun said: "I wonder what the Prince would have said if I had told him no; in fact I told him what he already knew, that Diana was a wonderful girl and that he was a very lucky man."

Like an excited schoolboy the Earl rushed off to tell his wife, Diana's stepmother, Raine, who had also spotted, with a touch of woman's intuition, that Diana was in love with the Prince. The Spencers, like any other couple, wanted to tell everyone about the engagement, but couldn't. The few people who were to be told that day were sworn to secrecy for the next three weeks.

Diana had asked for some breathing space before being hurled into the searching spotlight that would be turned on her the moment the official announcement was made; and more important, like any other young girl contemplating marriage, especially such a marriage, she wanted to talk to her mother.

Mrs. Frances Shand Kydd was in Australia, holidaying at her husband's sheep farm in New South Wales, and Diana needed to see her and not just tell her the news over a long-distance telephone call.

That weekend must have been an extraordinarily difficult time for the excited nineteen-year-old. She had told her father and her mother, but she ought not to tell anyone else and she was bursting to.

She really shouldn't have told her best friends, her flatmates, but what young girl could keep such a secret to herself? The fact that none of the three girls breathed a word during the next three weeks showed the great strength of friendship between all four girls. Any one of them could have made a fortune by selling the information to the papers, but they didn't.

She did it very quietly and with no fuss just before she packed her bags to join her mother in Australia. Ann Bolton remembered later that Diana walked into the kitchen and said simply, "I'm engaged." The noise of Ann and Virginia Pitman screaming with excitement in the kitchen was heard by nineteen-year-old-Carolyn Pride while she was sitting in the lavatory, and it was left to Lady Diana to tell her flatmate the news through the closed door.

"We knew how much in love the two were," said Ann after the world knew about the engagement. "But when she told us about the engagement, it completely threw us. We started running all over the place, laughing and shouting. Diana just sat there giggling at our antics, clearly thrilled by it all."

The four girls, who had all been friends since their schooldays, popped the cork on a bottle of champagne to celebrate; even Diana, who doesn't normally drink, had some. None of the girls had ever met Prince Charles, but they were to be honored guests at the wedding and were to meet the man who had been just a voice on the telephone. Keeping the secret during the next three weeks was to be a terrible strain for these three flatmates, but somehow they managed not to tell a soul.

Diana packed her bag, told them where she was going, and left for the airport on Sunday. She flew from Heathrow on Qantas flight QF2 first class to Sydney. She expected to be seen, but amazingly was not recognized until she arrived in Australia to be met by her mother and rushed off to the privacy of the farm.

Before long, of course, the farm was turned into a sort of mini-Sandringham, ringed by reporters and photographers—Australians, not Britons this time—searching for the elusive Diana. One newspaper even hired a helicopter to circle the farm in the hope of seeing "this sheila," as the Aussies called her.

Protectively, Mrs. Shand Kydd tried to get rid of the press. She even resorted to outright lies, not an easy task with all that scrutiny, by telling the newspapermen, "My daughter is not here. You have got the wrong continent. She is in the sun somewhere, but not here."

Not entirely convinced, the newspapermen gradually drifted away, and Diana was able to relax, even going out to a beach for the day, hidden behind dark glasses and a headscarf, to picnic and sunbathe. Mother and daughter had a long chat. Diana did not need to be told what sort of responsibility would rest on her young shoulders, but she did need her mother's counsel.

Since Diana's arrival the phone had never stopped ringing, mostly with calls from the press. The usual reply to any of the callers was "Diana is not here," but two days after her arrival one male caller was more persistent than most. "I am the Prince of Wales," he said.

"Oh, yeah, how do I know?" said the farm-hand who had answered the phone.

"No, look, I really am," said the Prince of Wales, making an early-morning call from Buckingham Palace. The tough Australian was not impressed and eventually Charles had to ring another number before he was connected to his fiancée.

Charles has a strong romantic nature and didn't forget to make another call to his sweetheart, on February 14, St Valentine's Day, and this time he was put straight through to her.

Diana had been sending postcards to her father and to her friends at 60 Coleherne Court, but she had given no indication of when she was returning home. Meanwhile, with Diana out of Britain, the hungry press corps had to content themselves with taking pictures of Prince Charles carrying out his official duties.

Her return to Britain was planned with the precision of a military attack. Charles realized that the attention of the press would be distracted by an event taking place on February 19; it would be an ideal day for Diana to come home.

February 19 was his brother Andrew's twenty-first birthday. The lad himself was currently training as a helicopter pilot at the Royal Naval Station at Culdrose in Cornwall, nearly three hundred miles from London. Quite rightly, Charles realized that the group of newspapermen who were assigned to sniff out his romance with Diana would be sent down to Cornwall to try to find out what Andrew was doing on his birthday. His dashing, handsome younger brother, only a heartbeat away from the throne, is a daredevil prince with a Casanova reputation as a ladies' man. Anything Prince Andrew did always made good copy.

Sure enough the pressmen set off for Cornwall just as Lady Diana boarded a Qantas flight home. She slipped through Heathrow Airport unnoticed and even went into London to pick up her car. She even slipped into Harrods to do a spot of shopping, but, unfortunately, this was her downfall. Although her picture had appeared hundreds of times in the papers, Diana was not instantly recognizable, especially dressed in a coat and silk headscarf like hundreds of other girls who live and work in the Knightsbridge area. But one person did recognize her, and she had a friend on one of the papers.

Diana drove down to Highgrove for her reunion with her husband-to-be. By now only one room of the future home had been decorated and the place still had no carpets or curtains. Charles and Diana spent the night in the bare but cheerful house before a log fire lit by the faithful Irish couple who guarded the estate in the Prince's absence.

There were up at dawn the next morning, February 20, full of joy, happy to be with each other again, little knowing the heartbreak and tears the day would bring.

The previous night the flickering light from the log fire had sparkled back from a spectacular ring. Charles had taken the large oval sapphire surrounded by fourteen perfect diamonds, set in eighteen-carat white gold, from a small blue velvet lined box and slipped it on to the third finger of Diana's left hand. It fitted perfectly.

Before she flew to Australia, Diana had picked out the design she wanted from a catalogue delivered to Buckingham Palace by Garrards, the exclusive royal jewelers. A man from the discreet shop went to the palace to measure Diana's finger. He didn't have to be sworn to secrecy; it would never have occurred to him to tell anyone. Garrards have been used by the Royal Family for generations. Even after the engagement was announced, the jewelers refused to say how much the Prince paid for his fiancée's ring. More than £30,000 is the closest speculation can go. A similar ring is on offer in the Garrards brochure for £28,500. Diana's ring, a rush special job, would have cost more.

On this bitterly cold morning of February 20, the Prince and the future Princess of Wales threw caution to the winds. Diana wasn't wearing the ring, but it was safely in her handbag in its presentation box. Charles decided to drive to Lambourne to ride his racehorse Allibar on the downs. The following day he was to ride the animal over the jumps at Chepstow racecourse in the fourth race of his part-time career as a jockey.

Diana sat in the front passenger seat of his blue Ford for the fifty-mile drive to Lambourne, Berkshire. It was something she had never done before. In the past they had always driven separately. Wrapped up in their joy over seeing each other again, the Prince had relaxed his guard against the press just once, and he almost lost the game.

As they drove unhurriedly along the M4 motorway to Lambourne, the press were speeding up behind them. The night before word of the sighting in Harrods had reached the royal press gang, who like to call themselves "The Mafia," as they were futilely searching the pubs of Cornwall for birthday boy Andrew. It was obvious to them that Diana would go straight to Charles at Highgrove. It was a long drive from the Cornish peninsula to Berkshire and "The Mafia" set their alarm clocks for 3:00 A.M. Arthur Edwards, a burly Cockney who had been chasing Prince Charles for most of his career as a photographer on *The Sun* newspaper, a tabloid which carried photographs of topless girls, was dozing in the front seat of the fast Jaguar limousine being driven by reporter Harry Arnold.

There weren't many vehicles on the motorway at that time in the morning, and Arthur looked up as they overtook a blue Ford that looked familiar. Prince Charles, the driver, looked back at Arthur in horror. Arthur couldn't believe his eyes; there beside the Prince in the front passenger seat was Lady Diana. Fortunately for the Prince and unfortunately for Arthur, his camera bag was safely locked in the trunk of Harry's car. As the duo from *The Sun* peered at the royal driver and his girl, the police intervened.

A backup car, a powerful Rover with a V8 supercharged engine containing two armed Special Branch men who had been tailing the royal car, swept up behind *The Sun* Jag, and with flashing headlamps and waving hand signals from the two worried policemen, the newspapermen were ordered to pull over. Harry put his foot down and the faster Jaguar outpaced the police. This cat-and-mouse game continued for several miles. During this time Charles was trying to work out how to avoid Lady Diana being photographed; he didn't want his carefully laid precautions against the press to be wrecked now, only days before the engagement announcement.

Using his usual shortcut through the back of the deserted service area, the Prince lost the newspapermen in the lanes leading to the riding stables. Diana went straight to the downs, which are private property and out of bounds even to newspapermen, while the Prince stayed at the stables, saddling up Allibar for what turned out to be a tragic last ride.

The Prince was in love with the magnificent horse, the lively gelding which he had bought the previous year for fifteen thousand pounds (thirty-three thousand dollars). It was his dream to ride the animal to victory in a big prestigious Grand Military Gold Cup race at Sandown Park on March 13. The race at Chepstow in Wales was just a warmup for that day. With a wave to *The Sun* team, who were still without their snaps of Lady Di, as they called her, the Prince, wearing a black crash helmet, rode Allibar up on to the downs for a seven-mile canter.

The Prince had finished the seven miles and

was just trotting up to where his sweetheart was standing on the edge of the downs when Allibar started jerking convulsively under him. Charles, realizing that something was wrong, quickly dismounted. He had only just stepped clear when the huge eleven-year-old suddenly crashed to the ground. Horrified, Diana, who had watched the whole thing, dashed over. The Prince was on his knees, his arms around the animal's neck trying to comfort it, but it was too late: Allibar was dead. The Prince was heartbroken; Diana, who shared his love for the superb-looking animal, burst into tears. Stable lads who were exercising other mounts on the same downs watched in amazement as the couple stood with their arms around each other beside the dead horse. The Prince, white-faced with shock and red-eyed, was trying to comfort his fiancée as the tears rolled down her face. It was more than ten minutes before they were able to pull themselves together enough to drive off to the home of the Prince's racing trainer, Nick Gaselee.

Twenty-four hours later a veterinary surgeon's postmortem report on Allibar revealed that the horse had died of a massive heart attack. There would have been no warning and the coronary could have happened at any time. If the horse had crashed to the ground during the next day's race at Chepstow, the result could have been very different. The Prince could have been badly injured, even killed, if the horse had rolled over with him still in the saddle.

Diana, her eye makeup ruined and her face

streaked with tears, did not want the waiting photographers to see her looking like that, so with the help of the two detectives and the Gaselee family a new escape plan was put into operation. A mud-splattered grubby Land-Rover was driven up to the side door of the cottage and Diana was bundled into the back covered with an old horse blanket just as if she were a criminal emerging from a courtroom. The Land-Rover sped off followed by the Prince in his Ford. The policeman in the brown Rover blocked the lane, effectively stopping the press party, who now numbered six, from giving chase. It certainly was no way to treat a lady, but in the circumstances her departure was hardly surprising.

The couple had planned to spend the weekend in secret at Highgrove, but with their discovery by the press and the tragic death of Allibar their happiness had been somewhat tarnished. Diana went back to London and Coleherne Court on that Saturday morning, leaving the Prince to go hunting with the Beaufort in Gloucestershire.

The Prince and Diana were to meet again on Saturday night at a formal gathering of the royal clan. Nearly all the senior members of the Royal Family were present for the dinner at Windsor Castle. They included the Queen, the Duke of Edinburgh, the Queen Mother, Prince Andrew, Princess Anne, Captain Mark Phillips, and Princess Alexandra. Diana went into dinner on the arm of Prince Charles. She was the guest of honor that night as the final decision was made for the date to announce the royal engagement. The

dinner had originally been planned to celebrate
Prince Andrew's birthday, but it turned out to be
a far more important gathering.

On Sunday she told her flatmates that the date
for the announcement had been fixed. It would be
the following Tuesday at 11:00 A.M. Over the
weekend Buckingham Palace told quite a number
of people that Tuesday was the day. Prime
Minister Thatcher, her staff at number 10 Downing Street, and some of her top cabinet ministers
were informed; so was the Archbishop of Canterbury, Dr. Robert Runcie, the man who would
perform the ceremony, and a message was sent
out, under great secrecy, to the heads of the
British Commonwealth all over the world.

In Fleet Street rumors started to spread on
Monday afternoon. Calls were made to Buckingham Palace press officers, who refused to reveal
any information. That afternoon Lady Diana left
her flat, carrying a small suitcase containing the
clothes that the world would see the next day, a
red velvet outfit with matching red stockings and
shoes and a vivid blue two-piece suit she had paid
£315 for in the ladies dress department at Harrods. At 5:00 P.M. she drove to Buckingham
Palace, where she was spotted and photographed
by a freelance cameraman who, with the click of a
shutter, made himself a small fortune. Later that
evening Lady Diana moved into the little room
that was to be her home for the next few months,
the spare bedroom at Clarence House, just five
hundred yards from Buckingham Palace. Clarence House is the home of the eighty-year-old

Queen Mother, who had readily agreed to make Lady Diana her guest.

Such an announcement could not be kept secret for long. The first leak came from number 10 Downing Street and by 2:30 that morning the second edition of *The Times* newspaper carried the news that Charles was to marry Lady Diana.

February 24, 1981 dawned cold but with a touch of sunshine to brighten up a drab London. The 11:00 A.M. announcement from Buckingham Palace, which was now common knowledge in Fleet Street and Whitehall, and the subsequently touching interview with the happy couple, would brighten the lives of millions that day.

Diana was up early. This was her first day in her new role as a future full-fledged member of the Royal Family. Her life had completely changed. There would be no more driving around London by herself in her little red car. She could never be completely alone again. The night before, she had been introduced to the armed detective who would now discreetly accompany her everywhere. He was Chief Inspector Paul Officer, aged forty. Officer was a close friend of the Prince as well as his bodyguard, had protected the Prince for the last twelve years, and had saved him from that attack by a mentally disturbed naval officer.

That morning at 8:30 A.M. he drove her, in the Prince's blue estate car to—where else?—the hairdresser. Diana had made an appointment with the same South Kensington establishment that had been doing her hair for five years. Owner

Kevin Shanley, aged twenty-five, who is also hairdresser to Lady Diana's two sisters, stood in amazement as Diana walked in and waved her huge diamond-and-sapphire engagement ring under his nose. "What do you think of that?" she said. "We all stood round in amazement and wished her the best." Kevin and his staff were given a real head start on the news, the first "outsiders" to be told of the forthcoming marriage.

Her thick blond hair washed and set, Lady Diana was driven to the palace by her new policeman. It was the start of a momentous and exhausting day for the teen-age girl.

At exactly 11:00 A.M. the Buckingham Palace press office released a simple, somewhat terse message, which was flashed around the world.

"It is with the greatest pleasure that the Queen and the Duke of Edinburgh announce the betrothal of their beloved son the Prince of Wales to the Lady Diana Spencer, daughter of the Earl of Spencer and the Honourable Mrs. Shand Kydd."

XII

What a Day!

Their joy was plain to see. In their eyes. In the way they touched and in the laughter they shared. "Blissfully happy" were the words Diana used, the light sparkling like champagne from the spectacular sapphire-and-diamond ring on the third finger of her left hand. "With Prince Charles beside me I can't go wrong," said the lovely teen-ager who was telling the world how she would become Princess of Wales and one day Queen of England.

On the steps at the back of Buckingham Palace, leading down from a stone-flagged terrace that overlooked lovely ornate gardens and a lake, Diana rested her head for a moment against the Prince's neck in a gesture of pure affection. He placed his hands on the shoulders of her vivid blue silk two-piece suit, and they laughed and laughed. High-spirited, like a schoolgirl, Lady Diana revealed that she answered the royal marriage proposal "straight away."

Diana and her Prince were pouring their hearts out to the world's press, whom they had spent the last six months so studiously avoiding.

The time was around noon on February 24 and everything was going perfectly. Earlier, sitting side-by-side on the sofa in the same sitting room where the Prince had asked for her hand in marriage, the couple had given an interview that would enter the history books as one of the frankest ever given by a member of the Royal Family. Then Diana and Charles had undergone an ordeal by television. Two tough TV reporters had grilled them about love and even the twelve-year gap in their ages. The unsophisticated teen-ager, totally unused, unlike her fiancé, to public appearances, had come out as a winner. It was the endless smile of pure happiness on the girl's face that really said what words couldn't and delighted the 500 million viewers around the world who watched that five-minute interview.

Prince Charles took the lead as they were interviewed, with Lady Diana giggling in a school-girl manner and at first playing purely a secondary role.

How did they feel?

"Absolutely delighted and frankly amazed that Diana is prepared to take me on," said Prince Charles jocularly.

"Absolutely delighted too, blissfully happy," said Lady Diana.

Lady Diana was asked when they first met. "I first met him in November 1977. Prince Charles came as a friend of my sister Sarah for a shoot. I never saw Prince Charles before 1977. I was always paired with Prince Andrew." Here she gave one of her nervous giggles.

When did they decide to get engaged? Prince Charles: "It was about three weeks ago, believe it or not, just before Diana went to Australia. She planned to go to Australia quite a long time before anyway and I thought, 'I will ask her then so she will have a chance to think it over so she could say "I can't bear the whole idea" or not,' but she actually accepted."

Lady Diana (with a giggle): "Straight away . . . There were quite a lot of telephone calls."

Prince Charles: "So many telephone calls from the press in Australia, saying they were Buckingham Palace or me. When I called, the man said 'How do I know who you are?' I said, 'Well you don't, but I am,' in a rage. It was quite difficult to keep the secret for three weeks but we managed it."

The wedding date? Prince Charles: "No date as such, but certainly the idea is the latter part of July, which is probably the easiest from all sorts of people's points of view. We haven't actually fixed the date."

He added: "It is much nicer to get married in summer."

The BBC man asked if he might dare ask about the honeymoon. "You can dare," said Prince Charles. "We don't know. There is a lot to be decided and worked out."

Where would they live after the wedding? Prince Charles: "Basically, I hope, down at Highgrove in Gloucestershire. I daresay that that means we will have to try and find somewhere in London to have as a base as well, but at the moment Highgrove. There's an awful lot to be done there . . . marvelous to have someone to take it on, organize everything, because it's completely empty at the moment—I'm just camping out—and there's a great deal to be done, isn't there?"

Lady Diana, again with a little giggle, agreed: "Yes."

Asked about being in the public eye, foreign travel, and public engagements, Lady Diana said: "Naturally quite daunting, but I hope it won't be too difficult."

Prince Charles said: "I am very much looking forward to meeting lots of different people," and a laughing Lady Diana said: "I am going to have to."

Prince Charles: "When I first started public engagements, think about the same age really, twenty, it isn't easy to begin with obviously, but after a bit you do get used to it. You just have to take the plunge. I hope I can help pass on the bit of experience I have."

He turned to Lady Diana and said: "You like people, which is a great thing."

What about their age difference—he is thirty-two, she nineteen? "Never really thought about it," said Lady Diana confidently.

"I haven't, I mean, it's only twelve years," said Prince Charles. "Lots of people have got married with that sort of age difference. I always feel you are as old as you think or feel you are.

"I think Diana will keep me young. That's a very good thing. I shall be exhausted."

After the TV technicians, the still photographers, and the reporters had packed up and driven away from the palace, delighted by what they had in their tape recorders and film cans, the future Princess of Wales found herself in a very strange new world. She would never be able to wander out and have her hair done again as she had earlier that day. She would never be able to pop down to the shops, especially the little late-night supermarket she was particularly fond of near her flat, where she would buy her breakfast grapefruit and milk. Worst of all, she would never be able to enjoy cozy evenings with her friends left behind at number 60 Coleherne Court.

That evening Lady Diana and Charles were able to get in the same car together for the first time without fear of being spotted. It was the end of months of secret meetings in country estates with high walls and long drives. They were able to proclaim their love for everyone to see. Diana had changed into a full-length simple silk gown, her Prince was in an evening jacket and bow tie, and Diana was still flashing off that stunning ring she was so proud of.

It was only a five-hundred-yard drive to
Diana's new home at Clarence House, there to
have dinner with the Queen Mother and her
Lady-in-Waiting, Lady Fermoy, who is Diana's
grandmother. It was a wonderfully relaxed evening after a day that had gone off so perfectly.
Diana was even trying out a sort of regal wave for
the first time, smiling and turning to a group of
elderly women royalists who had braved the cold
to stand outside Clarence House singing "Con-
gratulations and Jubilations" to the tune of a once
popular hit song by British star Cliff Richard. It
was a fairy-tale way for a prince to announce that
he had found his lady at last.

The announcement of their wedding brought
the vital news of joy that Britain, and perhaps the
world, needed at a time of gloom. President
Reagan and British Prime Minister, Margaret
Thatcher, were just about to meet in Washington
for the first time to discuss problems that spread
from massive unemployment not only in their
own countries, but throughout the world in general.

The dollar, the pound sterling, the German
mark, and the yen were all skating on thin ice.

Armaments, more ICBMs, more tanks, more
troops, higher defense budgets, were being talked
about in Washington, London, and Moscow.

In Spain the young King Carlos was facing a
violent takeover of his Parliament that was briefly
likely to take democracy back fifty years.

Détente was not working out—and new men

both in Moscow and Washington were making the dangerous decisions on how they would face up to each other.

For the superpowers there was trouble spreading from Afghanistan to South America, via Middle East tension and Far East chaos. And for the people relying on the world leaders to sort out the mess, the main task each day was finding enough work and money to either buy gas for the car or a loaf of bread, depending on which hemisphere they lived in. In Britain a potentially disastrous miners' strike was at hand.

Then at eleven o'clock on a springlike morning enormous joy was brought into the world with a handsome young couple holding hands and hugging each other on the green lawns of a huge private house in the center of London.

Sure, there were more matters of import to face the world—but here, at last, was joy. A reminder to everyone, no matter what religion, political view, or regime that love still existed. There was still cause for happiness. President Reagan and his wife, Nancy, heard the news on TV over breakfast in the White House. "Ronnie and I are absolutely delighted," said the First Lady. "I have never met Lady Diana but I have met her stepmother and I know they are a marvelous family." Canadian Premier Pierre Trudeau said, according to a spokesman, "Everybody is pleased, excited, and elated."

The rumors had been going the rounds of Britain's newspaper capital for at least six months, but when at last they could burst forth, the editorialists let fly with the joy that reflected the reaction of most of the nation.

The traditionalist London *Daily Express*, which has always been a defender of the Commonwealth and royalty, opinioned robustly under the headline ROYAL RAY OF SUNSHINE:

"It may have been the worst-kept secret in the world, but nothing will detract from the delight which the whole nation will share with the Royal Family on the engagement of Prince Charles to Lady Diana Spencer.

"His Royal Highness could not have made a better choice for a future Queen of England. She is British through and through and from a family of historical distinction and numerous Royal links. . . .

"A royal engagement and a summer wedding could not have come at a better time. The mundane facts of British life at the moment are pretty grim. The dreary statistics of unemployment and falling production, strikes and threats of strikes, have depressed us far too long.

"What better than a royal romance to warm and cheer all our hearts? All the world loves a love story and this is the premier love story of the decade. It will be the occasion of a genuine national celebration, and who will say that we do not need one?"

Another royalist and traditionalist publication, the *Daily Mail*, remarked, "Some Princes do have all the luck," then commented:

"At last, it is to be royal wedding bells. And we are delighted for them both.

"Prince Charles is a very lucky man.

"He has played the field and led the ladies a merry dance. And now he has been accepted by a lovely girl, who still has the freshness of the morning dew.

"Ah well, what's the point in being Prince of Wales if you can't do that?

"Dull of heart, indeed, must the citizen be who does not share in the happiness of Prince Charles and Lady Diana.

"Yesterday the whole nation seemed to be smiling."

The left-wing London *Daily Mirror* said: "Now we can look forward to a summer wedding. The bride will be radiant, the bridesmaids beautiful, the mothers tearful, the Prince, charming, of course.

"And on the day we'll all forget our problems for a while. Hopefully the sun will shine and even if it doesn't, who will care? We'll celebrate a splendid British occasion: a Royal marriage. The greatest show on earth."

The ultra-respectable and globally read *Economist* said:

"The monarchy is the main British institution that still works, chiefly because the British have learned when, and when not, to take it too seriously. While foreign republicans have to rally in moments of patriotic emotion round heads of state who—nearly half the population may be simultaneously shrieking—should be sent to prison for burgling Watergate or accepting diamonds from a cannibal chief, the British entrust the unifying role in national policy to a family supposed to derive its authority as head of British morality from its inalienable birthright . . ."

Then, referring to that great authority on not only British but worldwide monarchies, it went on:

"*Debrett* has discovered that Lady Diana Spencer descends five times from King Charles II, although four times from the wrong side of the blanket; but the real point is that British monarchy works well because its blue blood is constantly diluted by charm and fun."

There had to be at least one sour note, of course, and this came from the Communist *Morning Star* (formerly the *Daily Worker*), whose main circulation is beyond the Iron Curtain.

In what, one hopes, was a tongue-in-cheek article, it reported under the headline DON'T DO IT LADY DIANA:

"Lady Diana Spencer is to sacrifice her independence to a domineering layabout for the sake of a few lousy foreign holidays.

"As the future Queen of England she can expect a fair bit of first-class travel and a lot of attention, but with a £100,000 home of her own and a steady job as an exclusive nursery nurse, who needs it?"

The Communist organ of propaganda is not

usually among the daily reading matter delivered on the silver breakfast trays at Buckingham Palace, but that morning it was considered essential reading—for laughs!

It could not have pleased the *Morning Star* editorialists later that day either when the capitalist trading on the London Stock Exchange went up a few points with news of the engagement and the pound strengthened on the international money markets.

Obviously everyone loves lovers—even Zurich bankers.

And in the same way that what is good for General Motors is supposed to be good for America, the prospect of a royal wedding was obviously good for Britain.

On the London stock market there was a rush to buy shares in firms likely to cash in on the rush for souvenirs or in the hotel business. Shares that had been sluggish the day before leapt dramatically. Hopes that the celebrations would pull in more American tourists boosted the shares of hotels group Trust House Forte by 7 pence to 200 pence a share. China manufacturers Royal Worcester, famous for their commemorative plates and mugs, jumped 23 pence a share to 293 pence. Pottery and tableware group Wedgwood also put on 5 pence, while Birmingham Mint, famous for commemorative silver and gold medallions, jumped 17 pence to 223 pence.

Mr. Roy Stephens, managing director of Selfridges, the Bloomingdale's or Saks Fifth Avenue of Britain, summed up the feelings of London's store owners. He said: "It is good news for us because it will bring in a lot of foreign visitors."

A million extra visitors were immediately expected to pour into Britain from all over the world for the royal wedding, making it a record year for the tourist trade. An English Tourist Board spokesman said, "You probably won't be able to get beds in London for love or money before and after the wedding day."

The souvenir trade was likely to beat the record sales during the Queen's Silver Jubilee four years ago, when there was a boom in the sales of everything from teacups to bath towels, provided they had the royal crest or the Queen's head on them. By the afternoon of the engagement announcement, towels, scarves, crockery, and silverware, and hundreds of other items which some shrewd businessmen had held back in warehouses hoping with fingers crossed that Lady Di was the one, were being distributed through Britian by fleets of speeding trucks.

The leading soothsayers of the stars, the astrologers, also had their share of the action.

"Charles and Diana are a good love match," said one of Britain's leading experts in the field, Russell Grant.

"The Prince is Scorpio and his bride-to-be Cancer. Their sun signs are as compatible as love and marriage.

"It's the beginning of one of the most electrifying marriages ever."

Even a computer decided that they were ideally

suited. It also predicted their marriage is the one most likely to last. The analysis was made by Dateline Computer Dating—the biggest computer matchmakers in Britain. Information on Charles and his bride-to-be was fed into the computer and it returned the highest compatibility rating possible.

They were said to be ideally matched on scores of interests and hobbies ranging from sports to politics and romance.

So now we know . . .

XIII

That Princely Style

As he approached marriage, Charles was a well-rounded man. His main hobbies and interests were not just polo, surfing, underwater diving, flying, but also music, art, history, and archaeology.

He enjoys listening to and playing music. His tastes are mainly for the classical. His favorite composers are Bach, Mozart, and Berlioz. He has a passing interest in jazz and rarely bothers about pop. He used to be a fan of The Beatles because he thought they had an exceptional talent both as musicians and lyricists—''the more I heard of them the more I enjoyed them.''

He used to play the trumpet and the piano, but without great success. Then one evening he went to the London Festival Hall for a performance by the cellist Jacqueline Dupré and was so impressed by the rich deep sound that he decided to take up the instrument himself.

In art he prefers the paintings of the seventeenth and eighteenth centuries. He enjoys Rembrandt and Van Dyck and also has a fancy for Rubens, with all his fleshy ladies lying around. He does not have much of an eye for modernists, especially Picasso, whom he regards with distaste. He is an artist of no mean skill himself. When he first tried his hand at watercolors, he was taught by notable Norfolk artist Edward Seago.

His reading is mainly among nonfiction with only the occasional novel. Generally he tends to read history and biographies. History has great significance to Charles because he is so much aware that he is part of the continuing story of Britain. "I don't know whether it is me, or being born into what I was, but I feel history," he says.

He is particularly fond of the theater and enjoys almost any sort of play—comedies, thrillers, musicals, or the classics such as Shakespeare and Ibsen. London, with justification, is to Charles the greatest theatrical capital in the world. Given a choice, he goes for comedies.

Were he not destined for the role of king he would probably have been a very talented actor, playwright, or composer. His mind does not lean easily toward the technology of the age, but fits in easier with an artistic life.

On the question of food, he prefers plain English cooking but also enjoys good French cuisine. Charles likes a solid breakfast, and for lunch or supper, grilled meats, fish, and salads. He is not too keen on sauces. One of his favorite desserts is a good portion of creme caramel.

He likes the way-out, zany variety of humor, with a bit of slapstick for good measure. His favorite comedy show was *The Goons*, starring the late Peter Sellers in a British radio version of *Rowan and Martin's Laugh-In*. Up to the time of the comedian's death he often used to meet Peter Sellers and try to impersonate his mad antics.

Royal Sellers craziness livened up what was becoming a very stuffy and formal evening when Charles visited the Royal Regiment of Wales for the traditional St. David's Day celebrations in the officers mess. The Prince, as their colonel-in-chief, had called on them when they were stationed at Osnabrück in West Germany.

As a newcomer to the mess, he had to follow the custom of eating a raw leek and then burst into song. Instead of singing something very regimental such as "Rule Britannia" or very Welsh, like "Land of My Fathers," he chose a gibberish song made famous by Sellers.

Keeping a very straight face, he shook the diners into laughter with the "Ying-Tong" song, a constant repetition of the verse: "Ying-Tong, Ying-Tong, Ying-Tong, Ying-Tong Tiddle-I-Po."

Much of his humor involves poking fun at himself. When he was at Cambridge, he quite happily sat in a garbage can in a student-theater sketch about the garbage collector who used to wake him up every morning by noisily collecting the rubbish beneath his window. In another sketch, written by himself, he came on stage underneath an umbrella and informed the audience: "I lead a sheltered life." For one production he volunteered to sit patiently on stage while he was bombarded with custard pies in the old Laurel and Hardy slapstick tradition.

"I love imitating and mimicking," he says. "I enjoyed acting enormously at school and university. In a strange way, so much of what one does I find requires acting ability one way or another, and I enjoy it.

"For instance, if you are making a speech it is extremely useful if you can use acting techniques; I mean timing and double entendres and everything are enormously helpful. I enjoy making people laugh if I can and I always believe humor is a very useful agency towards getting people to listen to what you are saying."

His speeches show a brand of wit that clearly demonstrates he has a streak in him that forbids pomposity and stuffiness about his own role in society.

Just before he took over as captain of the *Bronington,* he told a gathering of the show business fraternity, the Grand Order of the Water Rats: "If any of you here are considering sailing on the North Seas next year, or you happen to own an oil rig in Scottish waters, I strongly advise you to increase your insurance contribution forthwith."

Speaking at a dinner for Latin American diplomats in London, he paid tribute to the area as "the home of the greatest games of polo and possibly the most beautiful women, even if I'm beginning to get too old to take part anymore, in the former rather than the latter."

Unveiling a bust of Prince Philip, he commented: "This does not mean that I am accustomed in any way to unveiling busts," and, as the drapes fell away, he added, "I now complete the process of helping my father to expose himself."

Humor in speeches he explains thus: "I've thought about it from my own experience. When I'm listening to someone else talking, if I get bored because they are not being amusing or something, my eyes glaze over and I'm not paying attention. I think about something else or go to sleep. When I see that glazed look coming over my audiences, that's the time to leap in and punch with something funny if you can. They wake up again and you can start again with the serious stuff."

He has an acute sense of what is ridiculous. When he flew back from training with the Royal Marines in Canada to be invested as Great Master of the Order of the Bath, he commented to his then secretary, David Checketts, "What I find amusing is that I come back after three weeks under canvas to become the Great Master of the Order of the Bath. Rather appropriate, I would say."

Practical jokes are also part of his comedy

armory. At Cambridge he often introduced himself as "Lord of the Isles" or "Charlie Chester," justified, he thought, because he was, after all, Charles, Earl of Chester.

He once went out to bat during a charity cricket match mounted on a pony and carrying a polo stick. When everyone was wearing name tags at a Royal Air Force dinner, Charles wrote on his label: "Watch this space."

He pulled a fast one on a group of American photographers when he was on board *Jupiter* and she docked at San Diego. The newspapermen were at the quayside to try to get pictures of the Prince. They asked the officer of the day to persuade Charles to come up on deck and pose for them.

The young Royal Navy lieutenant told them: "You're wasting your time, he's very pompous and not a very likable chap, you know. He isn't very bright, either, by the way. I'm quite sure he will not meet you, so you better go away and save your time." The cameramen walked away, grumbling, without realizing they had, in fact, been talking to their prey.

The impishness in his character helped to cheer up the barracks rooms of the Royal Regiment of Wales after that visit to share leeks with them in Osnabrück.

Some of the soldiers grumbled that because they did not speak any German, they were having trouble meeting the local girls. Charles promised them he would try to do something about their problem and a few days later sent them two lighthearted sheets of German-English phrases, which he and his secretary had compiled, with a vocabulary limited to the pursuit of women.

He likes to drive his sports car fast but takes great pride in believing that he is a skilled and careful driver. He never takes risks and is annoyed by people who do.

Charles is not one for discotheques, with their decibel-shattering noise, smoke, and shoulder-crunching crowds. Although, when he was in the navy, he would have boisterous runs ashore with the fellow officers. In Caracas he stayed until four o'clock in the morning in a nightclub with what Charles described as "a party of beautiful Venezuelan ladies." He also recalled; "As the ship sailed at six thirty that morning, I was not in a good condition at all."

A perfect evening for him used to be to take a pretty girl to the theater, followed by a quiet supper either at Buckingham Palace or in the corner of a discreet restaurant.

He likes parties but he doesn't drink much. He always says that he can get "drunk" on the atmosphere alone. At a party he tries to make everyone relaxed, to put them at ease, and make them accept him as just one of the gang.

Charles is not fussy about formality when he is relaxing with friends and acquaintances.

On one occasion an elderly knight who was entertaining him asked: "Would you like a drink, sir?" The Prince blushed and his host thought he had offended him by offering alcohol, but Charles explained: "I'm not used to being called sir."

He has a very few close friends he trusts completely, certain that they will not let him down by spreading gossip about him or telling any tales about his behavior when he lets his hair down in private.

Despite the friends, Charles until now led a fairly solitary existence. "In a sense, one is alone, and the older I get the more alone I become," he once said.

At Buckingham Palace Charles has a three-room flat cut off from the rest of the building on the second floor. It is decorated in pale colors and furnished in a leathery masculine style. The bookshelves contain mainly volumes on history, archaeology, and art. Other shelves have his collection of Eskimo soap carvings, including one of a huge musk-ox. On other shelves are eighteenth-century objets d'art, bought with the help of a friend who searches around the London salesrooms for him.

The Prince was always a bit fussy about keeping the place neat and tidy. He is apt to get annoyed over clutter.

Away from the polo field Charles also has drive and tremendous energy to carry out whatever he has committed himself to. He is a phenomenally hard worker. If he agrees to become a patron of some organization or get involved in a scheme to promote something British, he doesn't accept the job until he is sure he can join in wholeheartedly.

It might be charity work or a group to promote products from Wales, yet he hammers away at each task tirelessly.

As he says, "I don't believe in having totally honorary positions. If people expect me to become a president or patron and just sit back, they've got another thing coming. I like trying my hand at things and if somebody says do you want to have a go, I usually say yes."

His involvement goes down to the smallest detail. As colonel-in-chief of the Royal Regiment of Wales, for example, he wants to know whenever any of the regiment's soldiers are wounded on service in Northern Ireland. He sends them a large bottle of whiskey with a cheery get-well message.

It is customary for most royal speeches to be researched and written by staff at Buckingham Palace. The Queen or Prince Philip then usually puts the odd final touches to them. Charles writes his own speeches, expecting help from his staff only on the research.

He is always reluctant to express any controversial views in public, because he suspects that once they are recorded, they take on a permanence that can become embarrassing for him in the future.

His presence, he has learned, produces extreme reactions from some people. They either behave obsequiously, almost groveling at his feet, or they affect an air of pointed indifference. Charles considers the first to be unnecessary, while the latter verges on rudeness, especially when he tries to be friendly at all times with strangers.

"People always say to me, 'How boring it must be to have to meet so many people all the time?' I always say 'absolutely not,' because I find that one of the greatest advantages of my position is that I can meet all the most interesting and fascinating people in the world.

"I can learn a great deal—I always think one of the most important things in life is to be a good listener. I'm quite happily prepared to do the talking if nobody else is going to, but otherwise I find it very enjoyable indeed to pick somebody's brains and to really find out about their experiences."

He once summed up his life-style this way: "I do quite as much of what I like to do as is good for me, and I do quite a lot of things which are work, just as everybody else has to work."

He likes people to approach him. This is his style. "Yet," he says, "many nice people are too shy and overcome in the presence of royalty. Only the dignitaries seem to talk to me on welltried subjects, not of great interest."

He understands the difficulties of breaking down the barriers. "Unfortunately the nicest people are those who won't come up and make themselves known. They're terrified of being seen to be friendly in case they'll be accused of sucking up to me and because they imagine, quite wrongly, that I won't want to talk to them.

"I used to think 'Good God, what's wrong? Do I smell? Have I forgotten to change my socks?' I realize now that I have to make a bit of the running and show that I am a reasonable human being. An awful lot of people say eventually: 'Good Lord, you're not nearly as pompous as I thought you were going to be.' "

He has great energy for work and usually gets through the program of the day with the precision of a Swiss watch. He sets a rigorous pace. In Canberra he once roused everyone at 5:30 A.M. to go swimming sixty miles away by car. At 10:00 A.M. the same morning he was back in Canberra ready to start with the first official engagement.

While on tour, Charles often sips a glass of milk and stays up until 2:00 A.M., researching what to expect the next day, boning up on the people he is likely to meet. He does this thoroughly and often surprises someone with well-informed questions about their past that appear to be off the cuff.

He rehearses speeches with care and allows for passages where he expects people to laugh. When he stands in front of the microphone, he is word perfect.

Out of courtesy to her position he never refers to "my mother" in a speech, always to "the Queen." He is usually more informal as far as Prince Philip is concerned and frequently calls him "my father."

If there is an official program he doesn't want it altered—unless it is his decision. If there is a program, he will stick to it, and he expects others to do their part properly. A typical tour schedule is controlled to the minute.

In Tasmania, during an Australian visit, one of the organizers at an agricultural fair asked him to say a few words. This was not part of the schedule, but he could hardly appear churlish when he was asked so publicly over the loudspeaker system to address the crowd. He had no previous briefing to give him material for a speech, but he said a few cheerful, harmless sentences. He was annoyed, though, and in what seems to be a punishment to the organizers, he walked rapidly around the exhibits so fast that all the officials could hardly keep up with him, never slowing down to take his usual interest in what was going on.

As he flies around his mother's worldwide kingdom, Charles is very wary about getting involved in local politics. Before a visit the advance party, or the local embassy, assesses any sticky problems he might face.

He gets a run-down on the topics to keep clear of and any person to be on his guard against. Despite this, the need for the Crown to be seen to be absolutely impartial, some local bigwig is often tempted to rope Charles in to help him with a bit of electoral perfidy.

No matter where he is in the world, Charles has to keep up with bags of duty mail that are flown in regularly. His staff helps by sorting them out into readily understood batches. There is a pile for official letters of state, another for personal letters, one for the enormous amount of requests for him to lend his support to a charity or business scheme, while one basket contains just friendly, handwritten greetings from unknown, ordinary folk who want to send him a few cheery words of encouragement.

Charles sends his replies, like all the members of the Royal Family, on special thick paper called "Original Turkey Mill Kent." If it is a personal letter, he often handwrites himself, but usually one of the secretaries who travel with him types his answers. They bear no stamp, but are marked with the royal insignia on the back and on the front with the letter "E.R.," Elizabeth Regina.

Charles has to show interest, no matter how often he may have witnessed familiar fancy footwork in countless halls and arenas and heard so many conventional orations.

He stays bright, alert, and inquisitive for two reasons. One is that questing spirit to know about everyone and everything, while the other is the natural development of his royal training. A close friend of the royal household said of this aspect of Charles's life: "If you've been brought up to feel it's your duty to be interested in everything and everybody, after a while it's second nature to you."

A visit to Canada in the summer of 1977 was typical of how tough on stamina and patience a royal visit can be. Charles left London early one Tuesday morning on an eight-hour flight to Calgary in Alberta, site of that world-renowned rodeo, the Stampede.

Because of time differences, the Prince had

already added an extra five hours to his working day when he stepped off the Air Canada jumbo jet. It was only eleven o'clock in the morning in the prairie capital, while back in London it was time for tea.

Most of his fellow passengers went off to relax in hotel rooms and recover from the journey, but Charles began a nine-hour working day starting with a smiling, hand-waving parade through town. He took in lunch with some of the local worthies followed by a cocktail party for two hundred journalists covering the tour, and another round of formal glad-handing before making his weary way to bed.

Early next morning he helicoptered to a remote stretch of territory deep in Indian country where he had to be polite and look fascinated with the goings-on of such unlikely characters as Chief Nelson Small Legs, Jr., Chief Pretty Youngman, Chief Jim Shot Both Sides, plus three thousand other assorted Blackfoot representatives.

He moved in and out of tepees, showing the expected royal interest in a long lecture on the art of constructing these mobile homes. For the benefit of television cameras he mounted a horse and trotted for a hundred yards. The pipe of peace, which didn't give out any smoke in the Prince's case, was handed around, then Charles sat cross-legged on the ground while he listened to two hours of long speeches by the chiefs.

In pouring rain he carried out a tour of more tepees and, dripping wet but still smiling, he dashed into the shelter of a large marquee for an hour of traditional tribal dancing. Scores of colorfully dressed Indians stamped their feet slowly around a circle to the beat of tomtoms, the sort of scene most people see for just a few minutes in a Western film prior to the whooping braves riding away in war bonnets to eliminate General Custer and his men.

To lovers of native customs the monotonous thud of the drums and low moans from the dancers must have been very exciting. It takes a special brand of stoicism, however, to look interested and ask intelligent questions when you are soaked to the skin and once enjoyed the delicacy of the cello in student prince days.

Highlight of the third day was when the royal visitor donned buckskins and a long feathered headdress, had yellow greasepaint daubed on his face, and he was made HRH Red Crow, an honorary chief. Charles enjoyed the fun of it all.

On the fourth day, looking very tired, Charles changed from "injun" to cowboy. Wearing a wide-brimmed Stetson, cattleman's boots, and smartly tailored Western suit, he mounted a bronco and led the five-mile-long procession that opened the Stampede. He was joined by his younger brother Andrew, spending a year at school in Canada. As he was pushed, shoved, and shouted at among the crowds at the rodeo, Charles seemed relieved to have at least one familiar face alongside him.

At the end of almost a week of smiling, waving, rain-sodden dashing about, speech making, handshaking, and being pleasant to thousands of strangers, Charles went to bed exhausted. An American reporter, used to seeing his own president take on such a daily workload at election times only, commented: "That guy works so hard you'd think he was running for office."

As a Prince on royal duties Charles does his utmost to please people, and make them feel at ease, while at the same time preserving the dignity of his office.

Sometimes this causes him personal discomfort. During a visit to Papua New Guinea, where he was forced at all times to wear uniforms as requested by the government, it was explained to him that if he was not in uniform the tribesmen would not recognize him as a great chief.

Considering that the temperatures were shatteringly high, one could imagine his discomfort.

On the island of Bau in Fiji, he watched a two-hour long display of tribal war dances. Unaware that the Prince was not as used to the oven heat as themselves, the local chiefs had given him a seat facing the strong sun. He was soon extremely uncomfortable and had to fight against falling into a torpor, so great was the heat. His lips were bone dry but he never said a word. At last one of his hosts noticed his obvious, growing discomfort but unwittingly added to it by giving him a strange-tasting drink made out of grass roots crushed to a powder and mixed with water.

Despite the sour smell Charles gulped the drink back, though from the grimace on his face it was quite clear that this beverage would never figure on a list of his favorite tipples. He has often said that his stomach can take anything. On this occasion he proved it.

Outdoor life suits Prince Charles extremely well, and this explains why he has so much love for Australia. He feels he became a man there and that he will always remember those beautiful days of bush life while at his Australian school. This Aussie experience may explain why he is not frightened to speak his mind and how he feels that he should be regarded, warts and all, for what he is, not as the product of image makers.

"Images are dangerous things to cultivate because most people can see through any artificial character." He added in one of his jocular moods, "I suppose in some circles I could improve my image by growing my hair to a more fashionable length, be seen regularly at the Playboy Club, and dressing in excruciatingly tight clothes. This would, however, give my tailor apoplexy!"

He told a group of students in Ottawa: "The best compliment I like to hear are when people say about me 'Oh, he's so ordinary.' The most important thing for me is to have concern for people, to show it and provide some form of leadership." His concern for people was evident in his maiden speech as a member of the House of Lords in June 1974. He called for a wider education, the need for more parks and recreational facilities, a general awakening to "the challenge of removing the dead hand of boredom from mankind."

He pursued this theme more than a year later in his second speech in the chamber, when he called for more facilities for the youth of Britain. He is sensitive about the problems of young people and would like to see more organizations to channel energy away from street or soccer stadium violence into community help services.

Charles has never been inclined to become a leader of fashion. Sober, conventional clothes have always been his cut. He seems to follow the advice given a hundred years ago by the Prince Consort, to his great-great-grandfather, Edward, Prince of Wales: "A gentleman will borrow nothing from the fashion of the groom or the gamekeeper."

He shies away from flamboyancy. He prefers the discreet good taste of the well-pressed Savile Row area rather than the gaudiness and, what he thinks is the flashiness, of constantly changing Carnaby Street. His suits, costing five hundred dollars each, are made by Hawes and Curtis where his personal tailor is the doyen of wardrobe good taste, Mr. Edward Watson.

Charles orders his shirts by the dozen and ties by the half-dozen from Turnbull and Asser, the renowned blue-cottoned firm in St James's where the world's most stylish fellows clad themselves, at nothing less than thirty pounds (seventy-five dollars) a garment. Among other clients for their range of heavily striped shirts is film star Robert Redford.

The Prince's measurements, incidentally, are:

chest—thirty-seven inches, waist—thirty-one inches, and hips—forty inches. Weight—eleven stone (around 150 pounds).

There has been much criticism in England of his dress sense, though there was hope in 1974 from across the Atlantic, when Charles was on a best-dressed list. New York fashion expert Eleanor Lambert coupled him with *Kojak* actor Telly Savalas as one of the International Best Dressed Men. She paid this tribute, "For someone who is going to be a King, he can be quite hep."

"I can't help taking the mickey," said Charles when he turned up at a formal dinner of the Master Tailors Benevolent Association wearing a shabby sports jacket over his tails.

He told them: "I am often asked whether it is because of some generic trait that I stand with my hands behind my back like my father. The answer is that we both have the same tailor. He makes the sleeves so tight that we can't get our hands in front."

Charles may have been sluggish in the past over the sort of suits he chooses, but recently he has taken more interest in clothes. He has started to wear brighter colors with wider lapels and flared trouser bottoms.

One of his greatest pleasures is to go for lonely walks over moorlands or through woods. In the Scillies he wanders along the shoreline.

He indulges his love of an active, outdoor life by heading for the hills and grouse moors the moment the game season opens. Charles is keen on the gun and his standards are as high as his grandfather, George VI, who was out shooting the day before he died. He is rated one of the finest shots in the royal household.

He seems to have met everyone from cannibals to astronauts, from charladies to film stars, and his easy manner has made friends of them all.

During his tour of America toward the end of Jubilee Year he could be seen cracking jokes and holding his own in the razzmatazz of some of Hollywood's big names; he even managed to steal the limelight from superstar Farrah Fawcett-Majors of TV series *Charlies' Angels* fame when he met her. Charles also enjoyed a trip around the film studios, indulging his curiosity and his love of comedy by watching the shooting of the *M*A*S*H** series.

The ordinary citizens of San Francisco were as impressed as the film stars with Prince Charles's ready smile and friendly quips, when he took a ride on one of their famous cable cars; earlier on that trip, visiting San Antonio in Texas, he was besieged by a crowd of admirers who almost pulled him off his feet in their enthusiasm.

Texas provided another exciting experience when he tried his hand at cattle driving on the ranch of Mrs. Anne Armstrong, the former United States ambassador in London. He really saw some action when, with the guidance of Mrs. Armstrong's husband Tobin, he was shown how to rope and herd several hundred steers.

Visiting Hollywood and Texas, Alaska and New Guinea, is the glamorous, fun side of Charles's job, but the other, more serious aspects of his future are always at the back of his mind and for him they are just as exciting.

XIV

Housekeeping Bills

Saving pennies to make ends meet will be one problem that Lady Diana will never have to face—after marrying one of the world's richest young men. He already receives £250,000 a year and there is more to come. It will quadruple when he becomes King and starts to rake in cash from the Duchy of Lancaster as well, one of the traditional property interests of a British Monarch. The Prince is also in line to inherit a fortune of up to £60 million on the death of his ailing great-aunt, the eighty-four-year-old Duchess of Windsor.

But part of the strange nature of his role is that he does not get paid, either by the nation or the Commonwealth, for being the heir apparent. He must take on extra work to raise the money, a form of blue-blooded moonlighting.

Putting a price on junior kingship is something

that cannot be negotiated by trade-union leaders. There are no provisions in any known agreements on conditions of employment. Such are the arrangements in his case, though, that Charles's annual salary does not cost the British taxpayer a penny. To earn enough money to carry out his duties, to pay his living expenses, to cover the costs of his staff, his clothes and uniforms, his sports cars, his polo ponies, his entertaining, and his weekends away, Charles runs a complex but profitable business.

The main source of income is the Duchy of Cornwall, a rich property and landowning enterprise westward from London. He supplements this with other personal investments.

Unlike other leading members of the Royal Family, he does not receive any support through what is known as the Civil List. This is the system Parliament uses to pay the Queen and others close to her.

Charles is in the odd situation of doing two jobs. He gets no state salary, so he takes on other tasks to raise enough money to carry out his official undertakings. To earn his keep as a Prince he heads an organization worth more than two million pounds (over four million dollars)—The Duchy of Cornwall estates.

Annual profits average at £530,000 ($1,166,000). Half he gives to the nation and he holds on to the remainder as his annual pay packet. The rate for the job, then, is £250,000 ($550,000) tax free. It has been estimated that on current rates of taxation he would have to earn a gross of well over a million pounds ($2.2 million) a year to be able to put that net figure in the bank.

The annual Civil List pay for other members of the Royal Family: the Queen £3,260,000 ($7,170,000) plus an estimated £500,000 ($1.1 million) from her private Duchy of Lancaster estates; Prince Philip £160,000 ($352,000); Princess Anne £100,000 ($200,000); Princess Margaret £98,000 ($215,000); and the Queen Mother £286,000 ($629,200).

What Charles takes from the Duchy is conservative when compared with what the jolly, Paris-loving Prince of Wales of a hundred years ago pocketed as his personal income. Naughty old Edward, who did not reach the throne until the turn of the century, had a personal income from the Duchy of fifty thousand pounds a year. Allowing for inflation, this sum would be in the millionaire class today.

Until he was twenty-one years old nearly all Charles's income from the Duchy of Cornwall went to the British Treasury. The Queen was given fifteen thousand pounds to look after the needs of her son up to the age of eighteen when she then received thirty thousand pounds (seventy-five thousand dollars) from the royal lands to the West.

The total area of the Duchy is 130,000 acres, which makes Charles one of the biggest landowners in Britain. It is a mixture of farms and country homesteads, and old terraced houses, shops, and at least one pub in London. Its interests are spread over Cornwall, Devon, Somerset,

Dorset, Gloucestershire, and Wiltshire as well as all the Isles of Scilly. There are 850 tenants in the area of Kennington in South London, and thousands more elsewhere. If Charles visits the famous Oval Cricket Ground in Kennington to see a test match, it is also a case of the landlord paying a call, since he owns that green turf as well. Not much farther than it would take an Australian batsman to whack a ball, there is Lambeth Walk, made famous by the old Cockney song.

Kennington was originally known as "King's Town," marking the association with centuries of Dukes of Cornwall. This too belongs to the Prince.

Outside London his tenants include sheep farmers on Dartmoor, Cornish tin miners, and daffodil growers far to the west on the Scillies. He also owns the notorious Dartmoor Prison, a penitentiary most feared among the British criminals.

On the River Helford in Cornwall he has an oyster farm which produces a million succulent morsels every year, selling at around two and three pounds a dozen. Recently he subcontracted this operation to a big British marketing company.

Apart from having land on which hundreds of farmers are his tenants, Charles also has a 550-acre farm of his own. This is Duchy Home Farm at Stoke Climsland in East Cornwall, which breeds high-quality beef cattle called Devon Red Rubies. He takes a very active interest in running the place and helps Britain's exports by selling some of his three-hundred-strong herd to foreign breeders.

Among the odd perks is that any whale or porpoise washed ashore and stranded off the beaches of Cornwall belongs to Charles by ancient rights. In the Scilly Isles the annual dues used to be three hundred puffins, but these have now been reduced to fifty. He is still waiting to receive them.

The estates, together with the title, date back to the early fourteenth century. It was Edward III who created the title in 1337 and began the tradition of passing it down through history as both an honor and source of income for the eldest sons of monarchs.

Charles inherited the title when he was three years old, from the moment the Queen succeeded to the throne in 1952. The Dukedom, by tradition, automatically goes to a sovereign's first-born son, but only after the ruler has taken the throne. It is the oldest of such honors in nobility, because, until Edward III chose it for his six-year-old son, Edward the Black Prince, the word *duke* did not exist in Britain. It comes from the Latin *dux* meaning "leader."

King Edward's chapter instituting the dukedom is still preserved in barely legible old script in the British Museum. Fortunately for Charles today, King Edward regarded the young Prince Edward as his favorite son and showered him with castles and land under the terms of this charter. He was given the Cornish castles of Launceston, Liskeard, Restormel, Trematon, and Tintagel and other castles in adjoining Devon, including the mighty fortress at Exeter. With the castles came the rights to raise an income from all the manors, villages, and farms for scores of miles around the walls.

Over the centuries most of the castles crumbled, but the estates prospered, expanding into a wide belt stretching to London over rich farming country and thriving towns. Charles is the twenty-fourth owner of the Duchy of Cornwall. Over the years the money has flowed in but not all of the dukes had good fortunes as kings-in-waiting.

Ten of them never succeeded to the throne, including young Edward, the first Duke, who grew up to be the warrior called the Black Prince because of his habit of wearing black armor as he fought on numerous Continental battlefields. He died before his father.

Another, Edward V, was one of the princes murdered in the Tower of London before he had a chance to sit on the throne. The Duke of Windsor, the previous duke to Charles, was never crowned Edward VIII—he abdicated before his coronation. Several of them died as children before they could make use of the income or even reach the throne. Charles, so far, seems lucky to have survived the course.

The spread of the Duchy and the complexity of its affairs are enormous. Like the boss of a big business enterprise, Charles administers its affairs with the equivalent of a board of directors. To help him run what, in the 1980s, is a very up-to-date venture, there is an eight-strong Prince's Council. It includes some modern-day gentlemen with titles from another age, such as the Lord Warden of the Stannaries, Keeper of the Privy Seal, and Keeper of the Records.

The Stannaries title comes from the latin *stannum,* meaning "tin" and goes back to the age when a large portion of income for the duchy was from the thriving tin mines of Cornwall.

This quaintly named group go about their work in a mansion opposite Buckingham Palace that looks as if it houses a permanent, terribly English, afternoon tea party. The headquarters, with a permanent staff of twelve, is an imposing Nash-style building constructed in 1877. Such is the size of the estate that there are five suboffices spread throughout the West Country, including a granite fortresslike mini headquarters at St. Mary's, one of the flowery and windswept Scilly Isles.

On the board are some of the best financial, legal, and estate management brains in the country. His financial watchdog, for example, known as the receiver general, is youthful John Baring of Baring Brothers, the international merchant bankers based in the city of London.

Keeping a day-to-day watch on the assets of the dukedom is Anthony Gray, who for twenty years looked after the cash for the rich Christ Church College at Oxford University. As secretary and Keeper of the Records he is in constant touch with the Prince, advising him and receiving instructions from him on the running of the Duchy.

Charles takes the whole business seriously, ploughing into figures, reports, plans, designs, and laws on property ownership with enthusiasm. His estates are considered to be among the best run in the country.

While he was at sea, he still kept an eye on what was going on ashore, an essential chore if Prince Charles Ltd. was to continue as a viable proposition.

Mr. Gray, at the marble-walled headquarters, says:

"The estates are not really run as profitably as they could be. The Prince tries to be a good landlord and treat his tenants fairly.

"What he takes out of the Duchy is not much by today's standards, when you consider that this has got to pay for his staff at Buckingham Palace, all his living expenses, and cover the many donations he makes every year to charitable organizations.

"He is hideously generous with his money and hardly ever ignores a request for help from an organization within the Duchy. He gives away an incredible amount of his income."

The total value of the Duchy has never been properly assessed. Because so much of it is run as an almost charitable operation, not charging proper commercial rents, it ticks over, ignoring the true value of the rich pickings if it were put into the hands of hardheaded property developers.

Rents at Kennington, for example, are deliberately kept low to help the mainly elderly and poorly paid who live in the district. A visit from the landlord is not usually welcomed by most people, but when Charles visits his tenants, he is greeted with bunting and cheers. They decorated the streets for him when he last wandered around his Kennington property.

Among those he met living there were his former nanny, Miss Helen Lightbody, and a dozen or more other ex–royal servants. He popped into one of the local pubs, the Sir Sydney Smith, where landlord Alfie Goff offered to pull him a pint, but Charles declined. "I've had my fair share today, thank you."

Charles has a home next door to the regional headquarters of the Duchy at St. Mary's in the Scillies. It's on the very tip of England pointing across the Atlantic from the English Channel. This secluded hideaway, the cottage called Tamarisk, is alongside the offices of the estate. It even has an old cannon on the lawns, put there in the sixteenth century to fight off Spanish invaders.

Just a few yards along the narrow lane is the cottage, named after a wild shrub that grows among the rocks on the shore. When Charles helicopters to St. Mary's, he can mix business with pleasure by relaxing in complete privacy in between administering his affairs.

Tamarisk is an unostentatious three-bedroom cottage, looking from the outside like hundreds of other similar placed on the island. It has a huge lounge, an open dining room, a master bedroom, dressing room, study, kitchen, bathroom, and guest bedrooms. There is a half acre of garden landscaped with flowers and bushes. Passersby cannot peep in because it is surrounded by high walls.

One of the advantages of the island estate offices for Charles is that the building has extra bedrooms and flats for his friends and staff. To get there all he has to do is hop aboard a helicopter of the Queen's Flight and land on a football pitch three hundred yards away from his front door.

In accordance with the age of the title, Charles receives a handful of strange feudal dues, apart from the cash, as master of the Duchy. Among the odd ''rents'' are a load of firewood, a gray cloak, one hundred old shillings, a pound of pepper, a hunting bow, gilt spurs, a pound of herbs, a salmon spear, a pair of leather gloves, and two greyhounds.

These exotic offerings were handed over to the Black Prince when he used to ride down to the West Country for drinking, wenching, and hunting with his medieval friends. Six hundred years later the current Duke is still entitled to them, though armor-clad knights no longer hammer on the doors of the poor peasantry for these gifts.

He last received such tributes in a much less

rousing manner in 1973, amid the ruins of Launceston's Norman castle. Instead of frightened mobs fearful of more demands being made upon them by the royal gentry, there were thousands of happy tenants, watching a formal ceremony in which representatives of the various manors of the Duchy delivered their strange presents.

XV
King in Waiting

Although Diana will have to bow completely to the wishes of her future in-laws, unlike most other brides she will have no worries about the years ahead. A marriage bureau would describe the man she is marrying as having excellent prospects, to say the least.

What sort of future will Diana and Charles have as a King and Queen in waiting?

When Charles was about to graduate from Cambridge, he was given a booklet called "Choosing a Career." His fellow students may have found it useful, but he had no need of it.

The Prince's future has never been in doubt, and he has been prepared for his destiny. He is almost ready to be a king, and more than competent to cope with the responsibilities of monarchy. He has gone through the traditional training of an heir apparent—a short career in one of the services—and is now taking a bigger part in official life.

This king-to-be has been carefully groomed for the part, but unlike an actor, he does not know when he will have to go on stage to play the role. The date of the "opening night" is still unknown. There has been much speculation, though, about the possibility of the Queen abdicating early to make way for Prince Charles while he is still young.

The throne did not come to Queen Victoria's eldest son, Edward, Prince of Wales, until he was sixty. He became bored with waiting and turned to a dissolute life among shady friends and mistresses. While Charles does not show any of the basic character defects of Edward VII, it would be a pity, some argue, if he had to hang around too long before his coronation.

The Queen, happily, is still a healthy woman, pleased with her job, and as deeply interested as ever in the affairs of state. The constant travel and public engagements of the Silver Jubilee celebrations proved arduous for her occasionally, but that was an exceptional year.

Charles has dismissed suggestions that his mother should soon give up the throne in his favor. He sees no reason why she should retire. He feels that, because of the vast constitutional and political knowledge a monarch acquires by the time he or she reaches normal retirement age, the sovereign is then at a "most useful stage."

If the Queen lives to the ages of her mother,

grandmother, or great-great-grandmother Queen Victoria—eighty-two—it could be the beginning of the twenty-first century before Charles reaches the throne. No wonder he has forecast that it might be as long as forty years before he is crowned, though one does not know how seriously he takes this proposition. Yet his growing involvement with royal duties and an indicator of his future was dramatically demonstrated four years ago.

It was like a scene from a fairy tale, a Queen in a golden coach pulled by six white horses and a handsome Prince in a dashing uniform riding behind her in triumphal procession among cheering masses. This happened in London on the memorable seventh of June, 1977, as part of the Silver Jubilee celebrations marking the twenty-fifth anniversary of the Queen's accession to the throne.

Military bands and thousands of troops lined the two-mile route from Buckingham Palace to St. Paul's Cathedral. Hundreds of thousands of rain-soaked flag wavers from all over the world had hardly enough space to breathe, let alone to cheer and shout, as they crammed the pavements.

At the head of this procession to the thanksgiving service in the cathedral was a troop of the scarlet-clad Royal Canadian Mounted Police. Behind them were landaus and glass coaches, generals, admirals, and air marshals.

The Queen, with the Duke of Edinburgh sitting alongside her, waved to the crowds through the windows of the 216-year-old Golden State Coach. Riding in a place of honor just behind the right wheel was Prince Charles.

He was mounted on a sleek black horse just given to him by the Mounties. With a silver sword at his side he was dressed in the tall bearskin and crimson jacket of a colonel in the Welsh Guards. Across his chest was a lavish display of decorations. In truth, a suitable escort for a queen.

That he was posted in pride of place near to his parents signified the ever-increasing official role he now has in royal life. He is gradually taking from his parents much of the burden of public appearances and world tours. He is getting more deeply involved in the responsibility of preserving the Crown and running the nation.

He has also become a fully paid-up member of the more efficient team of national drum beaters in the world. The Queen and Prince Philip and Prince Charles are the salesmen of British exports. Wherever they go, they help to improve British trade with a subtle soft sell.

Preserving the Commonwealth is also one of Charles's great aims in life. He likes to think there is a family spirit about it, where everyone feels they know each other, that they have something in common. These come about, he believes, from a common language, common culture, common experience, and common history.

He has pointed out on more than one occasion that the Queen is no longer just the Queen of England. Thanks to several Acts of Parliament in

Australia, Canada, and New Zealand, she is also just as much "owned" as their Queen by these nations as she is the Queen of Great Britain.

This was the point he tried to make when he gave a confusing answer to a question during the July 1977 Commonwealth Youth Conference. In an off-the-cuff reply he said, "I don't think it would be a disaster if Britain withdrew from the Commonwealth and I am sure it could survive without Britain."

He was saying this to try to show the strength of the Commonwealth as he sees it. He also said: "I believe that the Queen, as head of the Commonwealth, is an important part of keeping the whole thing together.

"It is a wider family than it was and it is the Commonwealth and not the British Commonwealth. Too often people are inclined to treat the concept of the Commonwealth with cynicism, or to reject it altogether as an anachronism and complete waste of everybody's time and effort."

Two hundred young Commonwealth delegates gathered in London, from forty-five countries, were given a clear indication, too, about how Charles pins his hopes on them: "Above all I believe it is up to the young of the Commonwealth to show that they believe that association has something to offer the modern world, because without your support, interest, and encouragement, it will only be a matter of time before the whole thing fades away through lack of interest."

He sees his task as one who can break the

differences of color, racialism, political systems, languages, richness and poverty, to keep together what is still one of the liveliest international alliances in the world.

Charles is also helping to keep the Commonwealth idea of unity alive, showing how the throne can still act as the imperial linchpin. This is especially important at a time when there is talk of cutting ties with Britain in Australia and calls for separatism in Canada.

Charles has been trained for kingship in a period when society is becoming more egalitarian —almost antimonarchist at times.

During the Queen's reign the social order has changed at an increasingly accelerated pace, a phenomenon that the Queen and her advisers took into account in the training of Prince Charles. As a result he has developed a much greater affinity with student protestors, trade unionists, or the sons of garbage men, for example, than his predecessors.

The monarchy has been forced to keep in step with the developments in the streets outside palaces and castles. Charles revealed his awareness of the new society when he said, "In these times the monarchy is called into question—it is not taken for granted as it used to be. In that sense one has to be far more professional, I think, than one ever used to be."

Of the task ahead, he once said, "I've been trained to do it and I feel part of the job. I have this feeling of duty towards England, towards the

United Kingdom and the Commonwealth. I feel there is a great deal I can do if I am given the chance to do it.''

In the next few years he may join the Diplomatic Service, perhaps doing a job linked with exporting British goods. An appointment as a governor general of a Commonwealth country could happen now that he has a bride, and would give him and his wife two or three years of running a ''junior court'' before returning to Britain, and a possible coronation.

The only trade Charles has been prepared for is that of kingship. His grandfather, George VI, once said, ''We're not a family, we're a firm.'' Already he is a ''junior director'' of the enterprise, but unlike most bosses' sons, he cannot easily leave the family business. His role is preordained, unless he wants to cause a constitutional crisis like his late great-uncle, the Duke of Windsor, and abdicate.

He will take his throne at a time of changing attitudes toward monarchies. He realizes that the days of the aloof king on a golden throne are over, and that the continuation of his own inheritance is being questioned in the Houses of Parliament.

With this in mind he has tried, probably harder than any of his predecessors, to get close to the people he will rule one day. He wants to know how people live and cope in changing societies, what they are thinking—their ambitions, their hates, and their loves.

He once admitted he had no idea how people

existed in small houses or rented flats, or how they coped on meager salaries. His understanding is growing because he has constantly sought to meet as many people as possible from all walks of life, to learn how they hope to fulfill their ambitions. Prince Charles says frankly, "I'm not a normal person in the sense that I was born to be King. I have received a special education and training. I could never be a normal person because I have been prepared to reign over my subjects."

His popularity at home and abroad shows that he is succeeding in breaking down the barriers between palace and people.

He said after one trip to Canada, "I've been all over the world and I always feel how marvelous it is to come back to Britain. You can read the papers when you're abroad and you think everything is coming to an end. But you discover that things are going on the same as always and you feel happy to be back.

"These things that are so important we take for granted . . . our traditions and our institutions. This long tradition of basic freedom, which in so many cases doesn't exist in other countries. We need to be reminded of these very important essential freedoms, which matter more than any others, make Britain what it is to us, and also make Britain what it is to other people. All over the world people look to Britain for an example and a lead in so many different ways.

"I do worry about the future, but I think if one

can preserve one's sense of humor, ability to adapt and perhaps help to calm things down and to provide a steadying influence, all will be well.''

Whatever he does before his coronation, he is a well-equipped heir. No king in British history has made so great an effort to get to know so many of his future subjects, to learn so much about the countries he will rule, and explore so many different parts of the world.

When the Prince takes his throne with Queen Diana alongside him, it will more than likely be as King Charles III, but if he wishes, he could choose another name. A monarch is not restricted to the names with which he was baptized. Even if he sticks to his four Christian names, he could also be known as King Philip, King Arthur, or King George VII.

Whatever kingly name he picks, it is to be hoped that he fares better than the previous rulers named Charles. Charles I was beheaded in front of the Banqueting Hall in Whitehall one winter's day in 1649, while Charles II, the pleasure-loving ''Merry Monarch,'' is reputed to have died from mercury poisoning in 1685. He had a fatal tendency to meddle in the wonders of chemistry.

The line of succession to the throne after Charles is Prince Andrew, Prince Edward, Princess Anne and her offspring, Princess Margaret and her children, Viscount Linley and Lady Sarah Armstrong-Jones, the Duke of Gloucester, Prince William of Gloucester, and the Duke of Kent.

A youthful king would be popular both at home

and abroad. The Queen was only twenty-six when she came to the throne and there were hopes of a new expanding Elizabethan Age for Britain. For many reasons that feeling of a national renaissance slowly died away amid a shattered economy and disintegrating colonial outposts. Could a young leader like Charles, with his tremendous energy, put vitality and purpose back into the country again? Rekindle the spirit that his mother generated in her day? Provide a new unifying force for the Commonwealth?

Unlike the profligate Edward VII, Charles has had the opportunity to be trained for all the duties of kingship, and every chance to partake in royal affairs. He does not feel the frustrations that drove Edward into the life of a playboy.

While waiting, Charles feels that he can still contribute something useful to the life of the monarchy and the country, such as the work he did toward the organizing of his mother's Jubilee Year, or his active interest in young people's problems and the efforts he makes on behalf of Wales.

Since leaving the Royal Navy, Charles has taken the trouble to study in greater detail the constitutional role of the Crown, though he believes real knowledge of what a king can and cannot do comes from experience. "You learn the way a monkey learns, watching its parents," he once told the London *Observer*.

Charles feels that the palace is keeping pace, however, with the times, and the Royal Family is changing its life-style. Pointing this out, when addressing the New South Wales Parliament in Sydney, he remarked that it was not always easy to do this: "It is more difficult to adapt when the accepted patterns of life and society change so unusually fast." He thought, however, that because the monarchy was adapting to new conditions, the institution had become the strongest support of a stable government in Britain.

XVI

Lady in Waiting

Diana's second day as the future Princess of Wales must have been quite a shock to a teenager used to complete freedom. It must have given her a quick foretaste of the way the rest of her life would be mapped out now both as Princess and one day as Queen.

She woke in what was to be her new home for the next few months of her engagement, the spare bedroom in Clarence House. Outside she could hear the sound of hob-nailed boots ringing on the cobblestones as a soldier wearing a furry bearskin helmet and scarlet jacket, his rifle sloped on his shoulder, paced backward and forward in front of the house's black wooden gates. On the other side of the house one of the special squad of uniformed metropolitan policemen guarding the

Queen Mother was on duty, sitting in a small green hut.

A uniformed footman brought Lady Diana tea on a silver salver. The teen-ager was more used to getting up and making instant coffee for herself in the kitchen of Coleherne Court. There were a few raised eyebrows among the Clarence House staff later as the Prince of Wales's lady brought a touch of teen-age style to the royal household by coming down to breakfast with the Queen Mother dressed in a pair of her favorite jeans and a sweater. Not that the eighty-year-old Queen Mother noticed. She was used to having teen-agers around the house: Her grandchildren Viscount Linley and Lady Sarah Armstrong-Jones, Princess Margaret's children, often stayed in Clarence House.

Diana felt completely at ease in the company of her royal breakfast companion, of course. The Queen Mother had been a frequent guest during Diana's childhood and had often watched her play with her other grandchildren, Prince Andrew and Prince Edward. Another breakfast guest made it an even more relaxed atmosphere—Ruth, Lady Fermoy, the Queen Mother's Lady-in-Waiting and Diana's grandmother.

Over the next few months as the regal Queen Mother began to share a lifetime's experience of public service with Diana, preparing the teen-ager for the role she will have to play in society, the rest of the Royal Family would begin to spot the similarities between the girl Prince Charles picked for his bride and his much-loved granny.

Both are sweet-natured but strong, they are both the youngest daughters of earls, and have instant rapport with children, wild animals, and press photographers. Over the difficult six months of her courtship, constantly pestered by cameramen, Diana remained patient, cool, and polite. While Charles and even the Queen lost their temper with the constant attention, Diana alone remained calm. On the Queen Mother's eightieth birthday in 1980, Fleet Street photographers, normally the most cynical of men, spent their beer money on a beautiful china bowl and huge bunch of flowers for their favorite royal camera subject, the Queen Mother. All through her long years of public service, the Queen Mother has always made sure that the cameramen got their pictures. None of the other Royals, including Prince Charles, would ever bother that much. The Fleet Street men adored her and had started to like Lady Diana in the same way, especially as the previous evening on her way into Clarence House she had especially turned to give them a wave and a first-class news picture at the same time.

On this, her second day as a prospective royal lady, Diana didn't disappoint the photographers either. She had even begun to develop her own kind of regal wave, and her head was held proud, no longer the shy girl who was photographed so often on the pavement outside Coleherne Court.

It was to Coleherne Court she was driven this morning, her new detective by her side, to visit her beloved flat for the last time. In the rush of engagement day she had forgotten a few necessities. But she stayed in number 60 for only five minutes, emerging with a brown leather holdall before driving to Buckingham Palace for lunch with the Queen. For Prince Charles, meanwhile, life went on as usual. He was up at dawn, driving in his green Range Rover, dressed in a green tweed jacket, off to see a new possible racehorse to replace the deceased Allibar.

That evening Lady Diana dined with the Queen Mother again as royal household staff wrestled with the problem of how to address her. "We used to call her 'Miss Diana,'" said one of the staff. "But now all that has changed and we are not quite sure how to address her. She's much too young to call 'madam.' Perhaps she will let it be known how she wants to be addressed." In fact, the more relaxed "Miss Diana" continued to be used.

Diana didn't see her fiancé that night; he was in Hampshire on one of his fixed engagements, dining with officers of the 2nd King Edward VIII's Own Gurkha Rifles as their colonel-in-chief. The couple wouldn't meet again for the next two days as the Prince carried out his diary of engagements.

Late on Wednesday night the Prince flew to Scotland to prepare for his tour of a Clyde coast guard station the next day. On Thursday, as Diana was preparing to meet her mother, who had flown in from Australia, the Prince was in Greenock getting kissed by a pretty girl.

Throughout his years as a bachelor Prince, the

game of kissing Charles had become a regular feature of his duties. Wherever he seemed to go, in whatever part of the world—Australia, North America, South America, and even just recently in India—there always seemed to be a pretty girl on hand who wanted to kiss him. This time it was Anne Winton, age nineteen, who at least had the good manners to ask first. Most royal kissers just kissed first and asked questions later. The Scottish housewives packing the pavements outside the coast guard base shouted, "She's a lovely lass," and the Prince, wiping away the lipstick, beamed with delight.

Mrs. Frances Shand Kydd arrived at Heathrow on a Qantas flight and revealed she was one of the first to know the good news. "I am a very proud mother," she said. She marched briskly through a crowd of newspapermen, and when one photographer commented on her speed, she said, "I've got good long legs like my daughter."

That evening mother and daughter met at a secret rendezvous for dinner; they had a lot to talk about.

Diana and Charles were together that weekend, staying with friends in Cheshire and holding hands they went to Sunday morning church service; there was no need to hide anymore.

Over the next four weeks the couple snatched as much time together as the Prince's diary would allow for they knew they faced yet another long, lonely separation. That weekend Buckingham Palace released details of yet another long foreign tour for the Prince—this time to the other side of the world. Charles was to fly off on March 29 to Wellington, New Zealand, at the start of a six-week tour that would take him to Australia, Venezuela, and the United States of America. The Prince had long been tipped as the next Governor General of Australia and the British press saw this trip as a lead-in to an announcement of his new job, a job which would be ideal for a young married couple. At that stage there were no plans for Diana to fly with him in his RAF VC10 airliner. The couple would be back to the November situation of last year, late-night phone calls and letters. But there were plans for Diana to join the Prince in Washington at the end of the tour when he had been invited to dine with President Ronald Reagan on May 2. After that date the Prince's red leather official diary was empty for two weeks. Plans were made for the young couple to holiday together somewhere in the Caribbean, an island paradise where they could find some peace and quiet before the rush of the great day in July.

On March 3 they named the day—July 29, the place—St. Paul's Cathedral in the city of London. It was the future Princess of Wales who picked St. Paul's, simply because it's bigger. St. Paul's can hold several hundred more guests than the more usual royal marriage spot, Westminster Abbey, and it was Lady Diana herself—who suggested the cathedral so that as many people as possible could be invited. But perhaps in the back of Diana's mind was the thought that her mother's own disastrous marriage began at

Westminster Abbey, and she did not want to walk down the same aisle.

It was a royal first for St. Paul's, the first Royal Marriage ever to be held there. The immense task of planning for that day began immediately. Millions of people would flood into the capital for the ceremonial carriage procession from Buckingham Palace to the cathedral. Masterminding the whole event would be the Duke of Norfolk, who planned all the big royal events of the past decade, including Princess Anne's wedding and the huge thanksgiving parade for the Queen Mother.

Historians hoped that the switch from Westminster Abbey to St. Paul's was not to be an unlucky move for the royal couple. The last Prince of Wales to be married at St. Paul's was Henry VIII's elder brother, Arthur Tudor. But that was in 1501 in the old St. Paul's, which was destroyed in the great fire of London. The wedding was the beginning of a life of tragedy for the bride, fifteen-year-old Catherine of Aragon. Prince Arthur died five months later, and the Pope gave a dispensation for her to be married to her brother-in-law, Henry. A succession of still births and her failure to produce a son to carry on the Tudor dynasty led to Henry VIII's break with Rome, his divorce, and five further marriages.

At the beginning of 1981 the Duke, aged sixty-five, had been warned by Buckingham Palace to keep his official engagement diary free from mid-April to July 31. The wedding at which the new Archbishop of Canterbury, Dr. Robert

Runcie, would officiate would be a completely
new experience for the staff of St. Paul's. The
rest of the Royal Family, the Queen and Prince
Philip, the Queen Mother, Princess Anne, and
Princess Margaret were all married at Westminster Abbey. The Rev. Alan Webster, Dean of St.
Paul's, called an urgent meeting with the cathedral surveyor and members of his works staff
immediately. He was told the news in a special
letter delivered by an envoy from the Queen's
private secretary. The cathedral is capable of
holding at least two thousand people and the
British television companies, BBC and ITV,
would beam the ceremony and the procession to
500 million people throughout the world, even
behind the Iron Curtain.

The July wedding at the height of the tourist
season and just after the Wimbledon tennis
championships was sure to be a money spinning
bonanza for Britain. Hundreds of thousands of
foreigners would pack London for the event.

Lady Diana and the Prince would take a prime
role in the planning of their big day. Diana's most
important job would be to supervise the guest list
and, also important, to choose the wedding gown.
She hinted to friends that she was looking at
designs in pure silk and chiffon with a touch of
antique lace. The Queen went to the House of
Hartnell for her jewel-and-pearl-encrusted wedding dress in November 1947 and Diana's mother
also wore a Hartnell creation for her own wedding in June 1954.

Lady Diana's wedding ring will be made from

Welsh gold, of course. Could the new Princess of Wales wear anything else? The Queen, the Queen Mother, Princess Anne, and Princess Margaret all have wedding rings made from a nugget mined in Wales in 1923. The day before the engagement announcement Diana was seen shopping for romantic nightwear at that top people's lingerie boutique, the Janet Reger Shop in Knightsbridge. The shop sells pure silk nightgowns at a hundred pounds each. What she bought must remain a secret between her, the boudoir, and Prince Charles.

Honeymoon plans gave some headache to Buckingham Palace and the young couple themselves. Where do royal newlyweds go to get away from the world to be alone at last? What chance would they have with the world's press trailing them every last inch of the way? When young Princess Elizabeth married her handsome sailor Philip in October 1947 the couple tried to have a quiet honeymoon at Broadlands, the estate of the Mountbattens in Romsey, Hampshire. But hundreds of sightseers stormed the estate to try to see the couple and they were forced to move to Scotland for some peace and quiet.

The Royal Yacht *Britannia* was used by Princess Margaret and Tony Armstrong-Jones in 1960 and by Princess Anne and Captain Mark Phillips in November 1973 for Caribbean honeymoon cruises. The privacy of the royal yacht would be a good choice; so too would be the other hideaways used by the Prince over his bachelor years.

The couple seemed determined to keep their honeymoon destination a complete secret but the best bet did seem the Royal Yacht in the Caribbean with a stopoff possibly at the island of Nevis in the Bahamas. A romantic cottage with a four-poster bed looking out on to a palm-fringed beach was checked out by Scotland Yard security men at the beginning of February. Who really knew what would be Diana and Charles's secret retreat?

Meanwhile in the run up to her wedding, Lady Diana went to evening classes to take her first lessons on how to behave as a member of the Royal Family. Her teacher for the future Princess of Wales's first official engagement was of course her fiancé Prince Charles. The job he picked for her entry into public life was an easy one: a recital in aid of the Royal Opera House Development Appeal at Goldsmith's Hall in the City of London on Monday evening, March 9. The engagement had been in the Prince's diary since before Christmas and was chosen because Lady Diana and Charles both share a love of the opera.

Wearing what by now has become one of the world's most daring dresses, Lady Diana Spencer, the bride-to-be of Prince Charles, almost showed more of her bosom than anyone expected when she curtseyed to the other guest of honor, Princess Grace of Monaco.

This was the moment when international royal protocol decreed that the Prince's nineteen-year-old fiancé should be kept firmly in her place. While Charles was allowed to plant a kiss on the cheek of Her Serene Highness, the Princess of Monaco, Diana was obliged to dip in a curtsey to this wife of a head of state.

The fact that she had to do this to a former film star emphasized the fact that she will have to curtsey to many of the other Royals of Europe until the day of her wedding when she becomes Princess of Wales.

From then on the role she will play in international royal life will be very different, and Princess Grace and other European princesses will be her equal. Kisses on the cheek will become the order of the day when Diana meets other Royals—either that or a mere handshake or nod of the head.

In fact many of the members of the more junior royal houses will have to curtsey to Lady Diana after her marriage. In order of precedence she will be third in line after the Queen and the Queen Mother because of her new role as wife of the heir to the British throne.

Until then, as the daughter of an earl, there are thirty-eight categories of women who officially are senior to her in public in England (in Scotland there are twenty senior to her). This means that for the moment she must curtsey to all the princesses of Europe and above them down the line through duchesses, marchionesses, countesses, and the daughters of marquesses.

Diana discovered the next day at the breakfast table with the Queen Mother that her braless plunge into public life shocked and amazed millions. Perhaps the young lady did not realize how much of her creamy white skin she was revealing to the world by wearing that amazing black silk creation. Her dress became that day the second biggest talking point in Britain—the first was a savage government budget that raised the price of everything from gas to booze and cigarettes. To the British public, Lady Diana's cleavage provided a little light relief from the price rises.

Buckingham Palace switchboard was flooded with calls from the public, so was Independant Television News after their cameraman revealed a particularly close bird's-eye view down the front of the future Princess of Wales's dress on the late-night news.

Most callers, the female ones anyway, were adamant. "The lady should have been told to wear something more modest" was the general feeling. But the designers of the stunning, extremely low-cut black creation, which was made to be worn without a bra, were unrepentant. "We didn't think it was at all rude," said Elizabeth and David Emanuel, the young husband-and-wife team who were given a completely free hand in the design of the dress.

Lady Diana went to their Brook Street, Mayfair, salon the previous week after Prince Charles told her what her first public engagement was to be. She told the designers that she was going to a very glamorous evening where one of the guests was to be Princess Grace of Monaco. "I'll leave the choice of style up to you," she told the Emanuels.

The result made the large crowd outside

Goldsmith's Hall gasp with shock, and left millions gaping with astonishment at the TV. The news filled all the front pages of the morning papers and even replaced the usual bare-breasted pinup in a Danish newspaper. The stunning black dress was made from black silk taffeta with a fitted bodice and full skirt over a stiffened petticoat. The bodice, which was dotted with black sequins, was especially boned so that teen-age Diana had no need to wear a bra. The dress came with a matching black cape. The plunging neckline allowed millions of Britons to see that their future Princess of Wales was well endowed with a very full bosom.

Elizabeth and David Emanuel, married and still in their twenties with two young children, insisted "Diana loved it. The dress was very tasteful, exactly the right dress for the occasion. There is no way it could be called rude."

Another glamorous "new" member of the Royal Family was behind Lady Diana's choice of David and Elizabeth, the six-foot-tall, blond, and very beautiful Princess Michael of Kent, the divorcée who caused something of a scandal herself when she married Prince Michael of Kent in a civil ceremony in Vienna. Since the marriage the Princess had become famous for her incredible and extrovert fashion style, much of it bought from David and Elizabeth's small two-story boutique.

Diana, the teen-ager who had blushed a beet red when her legs were revealed six months earlier, didn't seem at all bothered about displaying most of her full breasts to the world. She was said to be delighted by the effect, so delighted that she picked the virtually unknown David and Elizabeth to make her wedding dress in preference to all the established royal dress designers, like the House of Hartnell and Ian Thomas.

David and Elizabeth, who greet their clients, even the royal ones, casually dressed in jeans and sweaters, just couldn't believe their luck. They heard the news on the afternoon news broadcast on the radio in the cutting room of their salon and celebrated with champagne. "We just can't believe our luck," said Elizabeth, aged twenty-seven. "We will make her into a fairy-tale princess for her wedding day with a glamorous gown which will amaze everyone, we hope."

The young bride-to-be will find herself cut off from her own family much more than other wives. This is because the Royal Family is such a close-knit unit, constantly supporting one another in their unique position in life.

Her future husband is particularly fond of life at home with his nearest and dearest, a habit Lady Diana may wish to break after a few years if she is going to establish her own home as an independent stronghold of junior Royals. Yet some of Charles's happiest moments are when he is with his family, whose sense of unity provides a welcome relief from the pressures around it.

When Charles is abroad he is in constant touch with his mother and father, brothers and sister, or grandmother and aunt, either by telephone or by letter. No member of the group does anything

without discussing it first with the others and
hardly any commitment is made without family
approval.

The Queen, who succeeded to the throne when
Charles was three years and three months old,
had also been brought up in a warm family circle.
The Victorian habit of banning the children to the
nursery and rarely seeing them until they could
either shoot or ride had long since died by the
time of her own childhood. Because of the loving
atmosphere she remembered with her parents,
she arranged that there would be no barriers of
governesses and nannies between herself and her
own children.

Now that Charles is getting married and
Princess Anne has a family life of her own, the
Queen sees less of her eldest children though the
Prince tries to be with his mother and father as
often as he can.

Every morning when he is in London, he be-
gins his day by leaving his own rooms at the front
of Buckingham Palace to join his parents for
breakfast in their quarters at the rear of the
building.

His mother's day usually starts at eight o'clock
in the morning, listening to the radio and reading
the morning papers and personal letters. Breakfast is at nine o'clock with Prince Philip and the
rest of the family. In the palace grounds below the
window, a bagpiper often plays a few cheerful
tunes to get the morning moving. Until lunchtime
the Queen concentrates on reading state papers,
dealing with official correspondence, and discus-

sing the running of the household with her staff. She holds audiences at noon and after a light lunch she leaves for afternoon engagements. At five o'clock in the afternoon she feeds her corgis—distributing the food into several bowls with a silver fork and spoon. If neither she nor Philip have any evening engagements, they often eat a simple supper on a tray, watching television comedy shows.

This will be the sort of life-style that the new Princess of Wales will have to get used to when she and her husband are carrying out royal duties from Buckingham Palace.

It will be a very odd world for Diana to bring up her children in. She will lose, in time, virtually all her friends from her free teen-age years. She won't be able to take the risk of someone talking. No one in the Royal Family laughs off a breach of etiquette. Diana will not be able to use her husband's first name in public and she will not be able to travel anywhere without prior arrangements and a detective beside her. She will have wealth and position, but at what cost? She will be expected to go with the Prince on the many hundreds of engagements he carries out each year from visiting shopping centers and exhibitions to planting trees. But she is likely to be spared military inspections and regimental dinners.

She will accompany the Prince on the two or three foreign tours he makes each year. Every moment of her time will be taken up with receptions, private meetings, walks around schools, universities, and factories. Her every move will be timed to the last detail. Guards of honor will greet her at every foreign airport or quayside. Her medical records will be sent ahead to suitable hospitals. Guest lists will be checked most carefully and everything down to who enters what room first will be set out for her by an ever present entourage.

Her husband will, in time, become one of the richest men outside the Arab world. She will live largely at public expense, never having to wash her own dishes, something she always did in Coleherne Court, will never worry about a mortgage or paying for her children's education, and she will have a choice eventually when she becomes Queen, of seven beautiful buildings to call home.

But the price is a lifetime of polite conversation. She must never appear anything other than beautiful, radiant, and gracious.

She will one day be Queen Diana, but she and Charles may even be grandparents before they are crowned. The subject of the Queen's abdication is taboo inside the Royal Family. If she stepped back for Charles at British retirement age, sixty-five, the Prince of Wales would be forty-two, his wife would be thirty—an ideal age. But the monarchy is not a pensionable post. If the Queen abdicated, the Royal Family could lose its almost magical hold on the British people. Majesty would begin to crumble; such a thing would be unthinkable.

As with the other non-Royals who married into the Royal Family, Angus Ogilvy, the Earl of

Snowdon (Anthony Armstrong-Jones), the Duchess of Gloucester (Brigitte Van Durrs of Denmark), and Princess Michael of Kent (Marie Christine von Reibnitz), Lady Diana was to be put through an intensive course in royal public behavior.

In the parade ring at Sandown Park racecourse on what was to be an unlucky Friday the thirteenth of March for her fiancé, Diana really was starting to look the part as a future member of the Royal Family. The Prince was riding in the 3.25 on his new mount Good Prospect, and Diana, flanked by the Queen Mother and Princess Margaret, went to see him saddle up for the three-mile Grand Military Gold Cup. Towering over the tiny five-foot figure of Princess Margaret, Diana chatted with all the racecourse officials and other jockeys like a real royal trouper where the rule is, a quick word with everyone. Occasionally the Queen Mother would give her a comforting touch on the arm as if to reassure her that everything was going fine. It can't have been a pleasant experience for the teen-ager with everyone staring at her as if she were a well-bred racehorse herself, but she carried it off well.

Her composure broke temporarily when the Prince took a nosedive at the eighteenth fence. She half stood up in the royal box and then put her head down, obviously too frightened to look in case her fiancé was hurt. She stayed that way until a tap on the shoulder from Princess Margaret assured her that all was well. Charles, meanwhile, was picking himself up, apparently unhurt except for a bruised and bleeding nose. In the unsaddling enclosure Diana was waiting to greet him with a hug and an anxious "Are you all right?" As "Action Man's" wife she will have to get used to a touch of nerves as her husband continues his daredevil antics.

She would soon be known as Her Royal Highness and she would have to act like one. For the rest of her life this quiet, non-snooty girl will have to cope with her every public smile being recorded, her clothes copied, and her behavior studied. Her life from now on will seldom be entirely her own. She must have sensed something of the loneliness she will face under guard in palaces and stately homes because she asked her flatmates to keep in touch. Leaving them her new private phone number at Clarence House, she begged, "For God's sake ring me up. I'm going to need you."

Dell Bestsellers

Love—the way you want it!

Candlelight Romances

At your local bookstore or use this handy coupon for ordering: